The Po

Leading With

Empathy

Overcoming the challenges
of leading in a non 9 to 5 world

ISBN: 9798799020941

Imprint: Independently published

The Power of Leading With Empathy

Overcoming the challenges
of leading in a non 9 to 5 world

By John McMahon

Contents

Foreword   7

Introduction   11

Part 1: The New Working World   13

1   Why Empathy is Even More Relevant
    in the New World   15
2   How and Why the Role of the Leader
    Has Changed   25

Part 2: There Is an 'I' in Teams   39

3   Start With I   41
4   Keeping the Balance   53
5   Train Your Brain; Teach Your Team   61
6   We're Surrounded by Distractions   71
7   Creating a Plan and Setting Goals   81
8   Reclaim Time and Productivity for You
    and Your Team   95

Part 3: Building Your Culture   **107**

9   The Where and When to Work Debate   109
10 Time to Redefine the Working Environment   113
11 How Do We Define Our Work Culture?   131
12 Values and Purpose   143
13 Hiring Aligned to Your Culture and Values   157

Part 4: Leadership and Listening   **173**

14 More Remote, More Trust and a
     Thriving Culture?   175
15 Developing Empathy Within Your Team   177
16 Communicating in the Non 9 to 5 Office   189

Conclusion   **219**

Useful resources   **225**

Acknowledgements   **229**

About the Author   **235**

Foreword

The pandemic and the new 'non 9 to 5 world' mean that traditional approaches to leadership are dead! John McMahon clearly understands this, and his impressive book presents a new and compellingly practical approach to help leaders support their people to thrive in the challenging modern world.

I absolutely agree with John that the cornerstone of successful modern leadership is empathy.

Why? Because it is the foundation of creating a high-performing culture. Let me explain more.

In Latin, 'culture' relates to agriculture and means to cultivate or grow plants and crops. The word can also refer to nurturing and developing people.

Like a farmer is concerned with creating the right conditions (e.g. the soil, the weather) for their crops to flourish, leaders need to focus on creating the right conditions for their people to thrive. Specifically, a first-class modern leader's number one priority is to help their people's brains to work properly.

If your people's brains are NOT working properly, they will NOT be at their best, nor will they be able to effectively communicate and collaborate as a team.

To help their people's brains to work well, leaders need to first show their people that they:

- Trust them
- Care about them
- Are carefully listening to their feedback and ideas.

Leading with empathy will give you the very best chance of achieving these outcomes. This book will show you how.

John McMahon offers an insightful and engaging study into how empathy became, and is continuing to be, one of the most important aspects of modern leadership and the undisputed key for leadership success in the non 9 to 5 world, our new norm.

Why should you trust John McMahon to be your guide?

When I first met John before he became a student of my "Tougher Minds" programme, he told me he had always had a particular fascination for leadership and what made people tick. He was also a firm believer that our brains and behaviour (thoughts and actions), and those of our teams, could be trained and changed to produce the very best versions of ourselves.

This desire to continuously learn, practise and then share those learnings are part of what has shown John to be an exemplary leader, having led his team at MCM successfully for the last 25 years, winning awards and winning business in spite of the many changes the world has seen in that time.

His humble and people-centric approach is very much echoed in this book. It also includes the views of many other expert leaders, from multiple industries, on how to lead in this volatile new world. It extracts their stories and unites them under one common banner of successful leadership so you can learn tried and tested techniques that will help you to empathise with your people.

Having worked with many world-class leaders over my career, across a vast array of industries, the lessons that John highlights in this book, in particular the importance of looking after yourself first, ring truer today than ever before.

It is my hope that any leader today who is faced with the challenges of a non 9 to 5 world reads this book. In doing so, you will be empowered to lead with clarity, confidence and a renewed sense of how truly joyous leading can be.

The age of the bulldoggish and uncompromising leader is over – it's time to embrace The Power of Leading With Empathy.

Dr. Jon Finn PhD, MSc, BA (Hons)

Author of 'The Habit Mechanic' and Tougher Minds® Founder (Award-winning performance and leadership consultancy)

To find out more visit: tougherminds.co.uk

Introduction

Imagine leading a team of high-performing superstars, who rarely bring you problems. They work together as friends, yet friends that challenge and inspire each other to do greater things. Each and every one of that team, including you, is excited and loving life both at work and at play, every single day of their lives.

Imagine being responsible for teaching and helping those people who are loving their lives whilst they also produce fantastic results for your organisation. Leading a team that works harder and more effectively than any other, at times that suit them, yet one that never needs to work overtime. Imagine spending your day encouraging and teaching, not disciplining and dictating. Imagine that day gives you a perfect balance between work, family, hobbies and health instead of constantly feeling like you're on a never- stopping hamster wheel.

The Power of Leading with Empathy will show you how this is truly possible and, what's more, how it can be a hugely enjoyable journey rather than a tough uphill slog. Regardless of whether you lead a team of three in a large organisation or a team of 303 in a company you own and run, everything in this book will either be instantly actionable or will help you and your team navigate the new ways of working that Covid-19 has brought us.

Sorry, you're probably as sick of that word as I am, but let's get it out of the way early on. For all the horror and terrible suffering the pandemic brought us, it also brought us a fresh outlook on life and post-2020 it is empathy that will now be the number one, must-have skill of every leader.

It's not a new skill, by the way. It's been around for many years and worked extremely well for a huge number of leaders. It's just not been particularly fashionable to admit! In fact, I only realised I've been leading teams with empathy for over 30 years now very recently. I always thought I was just "soft". I slightly envied those power leaders who could beat their chests and inject fear in all those around them. I'm not sure why though. It's probably because for years people said I'm too "nice" to my team. I give too much, I care too much and I focus too much on telling them to work less, not more.

But it has always worked. It must have. Our digital marketing agency MCM.click is now 25 years old and has the most hard-working, productive yet incredibly happy team you'll ever meet.

I get huge fulfilment seeing other people being happy and it just so happens that a by-product of happy, satisfied people is a loyal and incredibly successful team.

The New Working World

There's no denying that the world has changed significantly in a very short space of time as a consequence of the pandemic. Possibly the most widespread and irreversible of these changes has been on our working locations, hours and routines. Debates on the pros and cons of how much an office is needed and how often we need to be there will continue for many years to come. What is for certain though is that very few businesses will ever revert fully to the old style of working.

In this first part of the book, we'll look at how the working world has changed and why empathy is such an essential skill for leaders to master in that world. We'll also explore the role of the leader, looking at how that too has been changing steadily over the past 20 years and how this sudden seismic shift in work culture, and the expectations of those we lead, means that role is now changed forever.

Part 1

Why Empathy is Even More Relevant in the New World

Before we go any further I'm afraid I need to mention the C word again, because, unlike anything in our living memories, Covid-19 changed how most of us act, think and want to live our lives – **permanently.**

Our daily routines were forced to change in a very short space of time. Suddenly we had to adapt to working from home with very little warning and we did it, in most cases, with very little fuss or drama. We pulled together with a kind of Dunkirk spirit. Something that would have been planned, planned again and over-planned a final time took place almost overnight. We all had a common bond in being forced into lockdowns and helping control the virus and in many ways that brought out the best in people.

We expected it to be temporary but it lasted rather longer than we'd expected. And – shock horror – in the majority of cases the businesses that used to operate from offices five days a week didn't suddenly fall apart because their teams had to work from home. People didn't have to spend hours commuting to and from an office just for the sake of it. We changed our routines and filled that commuting time with new hobbies and time with our families. People bought dogs and moved to the country and actually started going on walks in the woods rather than around shopping centres. They generally didn't work any less hard though and many found their work time became far more focused and productive.

This gave us a new dilemma. Well, in fact, quite a few. Now the genie is out of the bottle we can't put it back, and do we really want to? Instead of people having to justify why they want to occasionally work from home, some now want their employers to justify why they need to be in the office. If they're more productive at home then why do they need to come in?

Then there are those who want to be in an office and miss the daily 9 to 5. They like being surrounded by people every single day and so what if it does mean they're slightly less productive? They did it before so why can't they do it again? But to be surrounded by people every day they also need you to tell the people that want to work from home to come back in!

Then there are the in-betweeners. They like people, they're social animals (we nearly all are) and they like the office, too, but they also like working from home. Oh, and they have a dog now, too, and their partner is being made to go to work in their office on

Tuesdays and Fridays, so can they just work on a Wednesday and Thursday in your office (because they also have a yoga class on Mondays)?

So, like it or not, the work-day routine has been changed forever by Covid-19. A shift to a less rigid, less office-based life has been slowly happening for years. The pandemic, however, accelerated this faster than anyone would ever have believed. Thankfully, few believe we will ever go back **fully** to the old ways of working.

As part of us learning to lead with empathy, this book explores the new types of environment that have emerged and why a less rigidly structured working world will have a huge impact on you and your team. We'll look at how and why you need to pay more attention to both your own and your team's work-life balance despite the new flexibilities, and how building a fantastic team culture outside of a 9 to 5 office routine is still easily achievable.

We'll also explore how – with more remote and hybrid working, less daily face-to-face contact and more freedom of hours and locations – we'll see the need for even greater trust between all members of the team (including you).

What was initially accepted as part of forced lockdowns will now increasingly become part of normal working life. Working from home, even if it's only a few days a week, will still mean the occasional dog barking in the background, delivery driver at the door and a cheeky faced child joining a Zoom call. The old expectation that you left your personal life at the door as you walked into the office has become defunct.

Each of us has a personal life, and it's how we as leaders empathise with this that will lead to greater strength, trust and cohesion in our teams.

Empathy isn't sympathy or softness, by the way. Sympathy, according to a quick Google, is, "*Feeling sorry for somebody; showing that you understand and care about somebody's problems.*" Empathy, as you'll see, is far deeper and far more valuable for you as a leader.

We mustn't forget that not only has the pandemic encouraged our teams to embrace and expect more flexible working patterns and locations, but it has also left an indelible mark on many. We have shared a common experience but how it has affected each of us is highly personal. Some of your team may have experienced a loss of loved ones, health consequences from catching the virus itself, fear for job security, financial hardships, childcare challenges, extreme loneliness, genuine terror and panic at the steadily rising casualties and not knowing when it would all "just go away".

Some of your team may continue to feel worried about leaving the comfortable safety of their own home, or have simply developed such a deep-rooted habit of being there that going back to a more regular routine outside of home may take time to relearn. You will also have team members who have thrived and found new opportunities throughout the pandemic, whilst there will be others who are desperate to return to regular old routines.

As empathetic leaders we'll need to manage both extremes, regardless of whether you have a choice as to exactly what hours and locations your team works in. If a decision from on high has been imposed on you then your team will at least expect you to know the reasons for that decision. You may disagree with it, and many of them may do, too, but instead of shrugging your shoulders and rolling your eyes, your role is to help them adapt and thrive in the new working world.

We have all changed at some deep personal level as a result of the pandemic. We have become more aware of what we were taking for granted, and yet there will also be a form of post-traumatic shock for many, both from the virus and the huge shift in their working patterns and the expectations placed on them.

This combination of changing lives, changing work locations and flexible working patterns, together with a very real desire from people to really appreciate and live their best lives and feel fulfilled by their work, means it's imperative that we listen to, understand and support our teams with empathy.

Making empathy your number one leadership tool will lead to:

- A team that feels valued, understood and trusted, and therefore more likely to engage and perform at outstanding levels.

- Greater staff retention and easier attraction of new talent as your team members never want to leave, so become your best adverts and recruiters.

- A culture that thrives on trust and therefore becomes more creative and innovative as people feel empowered to bring forward ideas without fear of rejection.

- Less need for hands-on management and more time for mentoring, sharing and teaching new skills and self management.

- Teamwork at exceptional levels because the empathy you demonstrate will become the norm throughout the team.

- Amazing levels of customer retention and growth as the team learns to treat their customers with empathy and, as a consequence, produce the highest level of service and engagement.

Empathy has always been key

Stephen Covey, the legendary author of *The 7 Habits of Highly Effective People*,[1] whose books have inspired me throughout my business career, summed up the magical effect of empathy by telling us: *"When you show deep empathy toward others, their defensive energy goes down, and positive energy replaces it. That's when you can get more creative in solving problems."*

Empathy is a learnable and teachable skill. It is a key component of Emotional Intelligence (EI), which the American psychologist Daniel Goleman brought to popularity in his book[2] of the same name.

Studies have shown that people with high EI have greater health and mental health, job performance and leadership skills through a combination of:

- Self-awareness
- Self-regulation
- Motivation
- Empathy
- Social skills

So, in the following chapters we'll explore:

- How the role of the leader has changed to one that needs to listen more, trust more and encourage others to self manage.

---

[1] *Stephen Covey, (2020), The 7 Habits of Highly Effective People, Simon & Schuster, 30th Anniversary ed,*

[2] *Daniel Goleman., Emotional Intelligence, (2005), Random House Publishing, 10th Anniversary ed,*

- Why it's more important than ever to focus on you (the 'I' in teams) and to teach your team to do the same.

- How to retain and attract the right team members by clearly defining your culture and working environment.

- Why it's important that empathy is the cornerstone of the workplace.

- How communication is the key to the strength and success of your team (both remotely and face to face).

I will be drawing on my own experience of running a marketing agency for 25 years and the insights I gleaned from interviewing over 50 internal marketing team leaders, CEOs and business owners, who have vast and diverse knowledge (from traditional leadership traits that will never change to businesses that have successfully embraced leading with empathy and running fully remote models with teams of 300+ since well before Covid-19 hit).

These included long-established names such as Princess Yachts, Admiral Insurance and charity Cats Protection through to innovators who constantly reinvent and embrace change such as G Adventures, World Vision and digital agencies such as ThinkJam and The Social Element, who have been running a team of more than 300 remote employees around the world for over two decades.

You'll hear tips and processes both old and new that will make leading your team in the post-2020 "office" both a revelation and a pleasure: a world in which you'll build an unbeatable team by leading with empathy.

Whether you are a team leader, MD, own a business or lead an in-house team will likely dictate just how much flexibility there is in your choice of working environment and flexibility on how and when your team works. Regardless of this, the pressure on you as a leader to adapt and empathise with the new needs of your team will be the same.

Not only will all of your team have been through the huge challenges of Covid-19, but they will all have tasted that once forbidden fruit of very flexible working. Your challenge is to listen, understand, share, teach and find a solution that pleases everyone from team to customers through to shareholders and accountants.

Leading with Empathy is the ONLY way for us to lead in the new working world.

Chapter 1

How and Why the Role of the Leader Has Changed

To lead well in the new working environments we need to shift even further into being a mentor, educator and encourager. We need to embrace some softer skills whilst also showing strong leadership and appreciating that people still need and want clear and firm direction.

Strong in-person leadership skills, however, are not enough to successfully manage the culture of flexible working. We've moved a long way from heavily disciplined and autocratic leadership styles over the past 20 years, but leading teams who are working even partially remotely takes yet another degree of transformation. You need to place a great deal more trust in your team, communicate far more purposefully and show empathy from a distance.

We know that when a leader lacks empathy a team will constantly be on their guard, protecting their own self interest; idea sharing and collaboration begins to decrease, people become more insular, small cliques form and a general level of unhappiness sets in. Much of this is far easier to pick up on and resolve in an office where the vibes from an unusually quiet floor, whispered conversations and simple visual clues that we all notice naturally serve as early warning signs. Even if your team is together a few times a week in the office, the natural signs won't necessarily be obvious, which will often mean the first you pick up on a problem is when people start to leave.

A changing environment

Recent years have seen a slow emergence of more flexible working patterns. Many companies permitted working from home on an occasional basis, often when deliveries or repairs (plumber, electrician) were due; others saw the potential years ago and have been offering remote working ever since. Some businesses went as far as to experiment with headline-grabbing schemes such as "unlimited holiday" and "four-day weeks".

However, the majority of office-based businesses continued to operate an outdated five-day-a-week routine, whilst viewing working from home or anywhere other than the office as far from ideal.

Numerous studies, however, have shown that remote workers can perform more effectively, are happier and have higher job satisfaction levels. One of the most commonly cited studies on remote working was carried out nearly ten years ago back in 2013 by Stanford University Professor Nicholas Bloom and colleagues.

The study was carried out on CTrip[3], a 16,000-employee, NASDAQ-listed Chinese travel agency where volunteer employees were randomly assigned to work from home or in the office for nine months. Those working from home showed a 13 per cent performance increase, improved work satisfaction and reduced staff turnover.

The problem is that for years there has been a stigma attached to working from home. Many companies have been scared of moving away from the tried and tested office-dominated culture. Reasons for this have included mistrust, fear of not being able to build a strong business culture and quite simply that changing to a more hybrid or fully remote model was too much like hard work.

Yet Covid-19 arrived and suddenly the world was working from home. What would have taken years of planning, testing, defining and adjusting happened almost overnight. The benefits of the likes of Zoom, Teams, email and Google Drive combined with fast home internet speeds meant the shift happened with very little pain.

Even as some kind of "normality" returns (if that's what we are calling the situation today), businesses are under pressure to offer flexible working on a permanent basis. Their teams are questioning why they would ever need to return to the old ways. The role of the office has changed forever, and whether your business hopes to operate a hybrid model

---

[3] *Nicholas A. Bloom, James Liang, John Roberts, Zhichun Jenny Ying, (2013), "Does Working From Home Work? Evidence from a Chinese experiment", Graduate School of Stanford Business, available at: https://www.gsb.stanford.edu/faculty-research/working-papers/does-working-home-work-evidence-chinese-experiment*

or a fully remote solution, the role of the leader has changed too. Modern day employees are unlikely to stay if they have a working structure imposed upon them. They need to be a part of the discussion, feel listened to and understood. They need to hear the pros and cons of each solution and ultimately will decide where they want to work depending on the environment and flexibility that's on offer. We'll explore this further in Chapter 9.

The new working models

Offices are highly unlikely to disappear completely and will still have many benefits, but many will cease to have rows of desks and chairs that the same individuals sit in day in, day out. They will also cease to be as large, and maybe won't need to be in the most expensive locations. They will be shared workspaces, social hubs and collaborative centres to generate ideas. Throughout this book I refer to several types of work environments.

For clarity, this is the terminology I use throughout the rest of this book:

Office '9 to 5': You are expected to go to an office daily for a set number of hours. Working away from the office is an exception rather than the rule.

Hybrid working: This is usually the term used when people are slightly scared of ditching the old 9 to 5, but recognise that people will want much greater flexibility. We'll explore the dangers of this later. This is a much-used term at the time of writing, one I believe is fraught with danger due to its lack of clear policy.

Work from anywhere (WFA): Your team can work from anywhere in the world but agree to attend face-to-face meetings weekly, quarterly or annually. They also agree they will be present virtually at all other meetings as requested. The WFA model usually has hubs that the team can attend for meetings or work at if they don't want to work from home. Alternatively they provide the funds for team members to work from shared offices close to their homes.

Fully remote: Everyone works remotely. There is no office. Face-to-face meetups are generally once or twice a year (if at all).

So, unless you are definitely sticking with 9 to 5 (in which case you might not want to read the rest of this book!), the blurred lines between work and life will remain. We will need to be far stronger willed and more disciplined than ever before. Author Simon Sinek, in his book *Leaders Eat Last*[4], quite rightly says a leader needs to put others ahead of themself. Leadership no longer only comes with a title though, you need to get people's permission to lead them; to do that you need to lead with empathy.

---

[4] *Simon Sinek, (2017), Leaders Eat Last: Why Some Teams Pull Together and Others Don't, Penguin*

You engage a team via humour and humility

If you, as a leader, are also new to hybrid or remote working, stepping into this new world may feel challenging and you may be unsure of the best approach to take. However, empathy provides the answer.

The hybrid or remote leader needs to be alert to the feelings and situation of the team at all times at a much deeper level than before. If our own work-life balance has changed and the blur between the two has increased, then it certainly has for our teams as well.

Empathy, as we know, is the ability to sense and understand another person's emotions whilst seeing things from their perspective. As a leader it's about putting yourself in someone else's shoes, connecting and communicating, inspiring and, above all else, listening.

It's also about admitting we're all human and sharing our own mistakes and challenges - something that may have felt like a display of weakness before. The serious, indestructible and untiring leader is now far less likely to be able to connect and inspire their team than one who shows their true self.

During my interviews for this book Kiran Haslam, Chief Marketing Officer at Princess Yachts, told me: *"You engage a team via humour and humility. You can't take yourself too seriously; that's the secret. To make sure you get it right, look at how you impact the people and the world around you."*

Kiran also pointed out how video meetings have broken down some of the barriers, making it easier to empathise with people. We have a physical view into each other's homes; we hear dogs barking and washing machines whirring in the background. It's no longer frowned upon to have a doorbell ring or a delivery arrive. We're inviting people into our homes and our personal lives rather than just seeing the professional face we show at the office. This can actually work as a positive for strengthening bonds and connecting on a deeper level.

However, much of this interaction has to be far more scheduled and planned than spontaneously wandering around the office, picking up on conversations and having informal chats. Keeping the constant communication loop open is one of the key challenges remote or hybrid leaders will need to overcome. It requires a new skill set, and will be more of a change than many realise.

You have a full schedule already but remote communication will take even more of that time and demand careful planning and consistency. Simultaneously, you'll need to ensure that something that once happened naturally and by chance face to face doesn't lose authenticity when it's planned.

Being an empathetic, non 9 to 5 leader is not about appearing strong and charismatic as you inspire the troops. Hybrid teams need you to be organised and productive and to help them be the same. They also need you to help them facilitate connections within the team (and to keep that natural yet collaborative and human).

Communication also means being open and honest in every area of your organisation (an important part of the working culture that we'll discuss further in Chapter 11).

Never assume that your team knows the direction and plan at all times. I've made this mistake many times before. It's easy to sit in planning sessions with your leadership team, consultants or specialist groups, come away fired up and inspired to take action, get sucked back into the day-to-day tasks, implement the new plans and then assume the entire team knows why they're in place or why there's a change in direction. This trap becomes even easier to fall into when your whole team is scattered between locations.

Two-way communication is key

Remember that it's now even more crucial that this communication goes two ways. Listening (and wanting to listen) could be your best tool to build a strong team, and encouraging them to listen is equally important!

Above all, you need to have and help build trust: trust in you as a leader, trust between the team members and crucially you need to be able to trust your team. Trust has always been central to team cohesion and function but when people are out of view and not surrounded by colleagues, it is essential that you have a culture of trust that never questions the work ethics of others. Timesheets do still have their use in some areas for billing or productivity, but if letting people work remotely means timesheets or, far worse, real-time monitoring tools to check they're working hard then you will soon have an extremely dysfunctional team.

Trust in you will not only be built by demonstration of your skills, productivity and always acting on your word, but also by showing you're not infallible. Transparency is key. Showing people that you make mistakes from time to time isn't a sign of weakness. If you want to keep people active and constantly bringing new ideas then you need to admit that many of your ideas don't work: "*I had an idea, it didn't work, it turned out not to be a great idea, here's why I thought it would work and here's why it didn't,*" demonstrates that it's OK to keep trying (provided we learn as we go along).

Is a team a family?

We've always described our team as a family at MCM. I've always felt that's a slightly cheesy description but it's true of the way we communicate and work on so many levels. The family may have its disagreements from time to time, may have the odd sulk and stamp of feet, but great bonds are formed and trust grows from those bonds. We learn from each other and we point out where we go wrong, but not in a spiteful way. On the inside we can show each other and help each other to build on and conquer our weaknesses then, just like a family, the minute we leave the front door we're a strong and indivisible unit grinning from ear to ear!

This family atmosphere then filters down to the clients and they love working with us. Kiran at Princess Yachts describes that sense of family in a high-performing team as the "family feel" but "not in an American way!'" All the benefits and none of the cheese?!

Tamara Littleton, CEO of The Social Element, an agency that was started with a remote model but now employs over 300 people around the world, told me: *"We focus on getting that sense of team, so they all know each other; they can be vulnerable with each other, they can trust each other and hold each other accountable. So that's been a massive influence for us on the culture. Oh and I'm quite happy to admit when I've messed up, or taken the company in a different direction, and say, 'Oh, that didn't work, did it?'"*

The role of the leader has changed for most businesses whether you are 9 to 5 or flexible working. The core elements and skill sets remain, but the focus for anyone leading a non 9 to 5 team now has to rest far more heavily on the facilitation and building of:

- Trust
- Transparency
- Organisation skills
- Communication

All of these skills (as we will discuss later) will only be maintained, grown and perfected by mastering the fourth one, communication. Many areas of communication that we once took for granted in a regular face-to-face environment now need careful crafting and continuous attention. It is a skill that requires planning, dedication, reliable repetition, enthusiasm and, above all, empathy.

Mark Pearson, now of The Marketing Centre, told me that over 20 years ago, when he was head of brand for the industry-transforming bank Egg, the team there was already making the most of hybrid working – most of it fully remote. Incredibly they were making it work despite the excruciatingly slow dial-up internet speed available then. We now take for granted the huge benefits of Zoom, Teams, Slack, and a whole host of platforms – even if many of us also have a love-hate relationship with them!

You are no longer carrying passengers

The old analogy that as a leader you are the driver of the bus picking up your team passengers and driving them to the destination has changed. Of course you still need the right people on board with you, but now you need to help them learn to drive their own vehicles alongside you.

Empathetic leadership means teaching and encouraging, not dictating and bullying. Helping people to learn and feel valued and more fulfilled in what they are doing means they constantly want to do better, and people soon begin to crave new skills and knowledge rather than being fearful of putting a foot wrong. Soon people are teaching each other, feeding off each other's encouragement and achievements and, as a result, your job as a leader becomes far easier and more fulfilling as you watch the team 'self grow.'

The snowmobile replaces the bus

A few years ago I met Dr Jon Finn BA (Hons), MSc, PhD and founder of Tougher Minds[5], an award-winning consultancy that has helped some of the country's premier sports teams and businesses become world class through the study and continuous training of science-based brain training and personal development skills.

He describes leading as "every individual on your team is driving a snowmobile". The team can be seen as a fleet of snowmobiles aiming to reach the summit of a mountain. The conditions are constantly changing and it's the leader's job to make sure everyone on the team becomes really good at driving their snowmobile in these challenging conditions.

Driving conditions

We all know just how much conditions changed in 2020, and trying to keep teaching your team to drive when you're actually learning to adapt your driving skills yourself is even more of a challenge.

The great thing is this new way of leading means being comfortable showing your team that you're learning too and aren't uncomfortable making mistakes. If your snowmobile suddenly swerves left and lands perilously close to the edge, as mine undoubtedly would in a real snowmobile, be prepared for people to see. Then tell them what you did that they shouldn't do. If everyone on your team learns to share

---

[5] *www.tougherminds.co.uk*

mistakes and ask for guidance, the team continues to grow and bond.

Teaching your team how to adapt to new working habits, keep at their most productive, be their best, their happiest and their healthiest to enable them to excel at their roles, and at the same time learning with them is an essential part of leading with empathy in the non 9 to 5 world. Putting more focus on them achieving happiness and healthiness, and genuinely wanting them to achieve that ideal work-life balance, will mean the productivity and results for the business will be a natural consequence.

The new normal

It is now an undisputed fact that working locations, hours and culture are changing permanently, whether we fight against it or not. The genie is out of the bottle; our staff know that it's possible for them to work from home effectively, and often more effectively, whilst also achieving a much better work-life balance. Instead of them requesting flexible working, we, as leaders, are being asked to justify why we would insist on a return to the old fashioned 9 to 5.

Choosing to evolve as an empathetic and focused leader puts you in a position of strength, and will enable you to promote a positive culture with a welcome work-life balance.

There Is an 'I' in Teams

The empathetic leader must be resilient yet sympathetic, driven yet understanding, and none of this can be achieved if you are stressed and burning out. You need to be the best version of yourself in order to help your team to be the same and that means starting with you, because there is an "I" in teams and that "I" is you.

In this part of the book, I'll explore how the role of the leader has shifted and why the old adage of *"there is no 'I' in teams"* may be wrong and no longer part of our future.

By the end of this section, you'll know how to manage the distractions that threaten to derail your team, deal with the ongoing onslaught of electronic communication and protect yourself and your team from digital burnout.

It's time to define the working practices we want to create, set achievable goals to reach them and, most of all, lead your team with empathy.

Part 2

Start With I

I'm sure you've heard the phrase: "*There is no 'I' in teams.*" It's thought to have first been used by sports coaches encouraging players to work together, recognise each other's skills, not hog the ball and use their combined talents to win.

When applied to work colleagues and teams it's easy to see why this phrase has always had so much relevance. The very best teams have a whole mixture of skill sets, and combining these through cooperation, trust, mutual appreciation, healthy conflict and debate can bring far better results than one person alone.

Personal excellence

However, if each individual in that team doesn't focus first on excelling at what they do, how they live and how they act, they won't make a great contribution to any team. It's said that the late and legendary National Basketball Association player

Kobe Bryant was once accused of hogging the ball by his team-mates. One of the team, Shaq O'Neal, apparently volunteered to have a word with him. He says he told him: "Kobe, *there's no 'I' in Team.*" to which Kobe replied, "*I know. But there's an 'M' and an 'E' in that, motherf*****.*"

Be your best version of yourself

Only by focusing on being the best version of yourself first can you then go on to coach and mentor each individual in the team to focus on finding and becoming their best versions of themselves too. This may go against many mantras we've been taught about teamwork in the past, but continuing to believe that there is no "I" in a team and forgetting to focus on yourself is fraught with danger.

As leaders it's easy to focus our energy on making sure others are highly functioning, and all too quickly we fall into the trap of not taking our own advice.

Many of the leaders I've spoken to over the past year have been noticeably uncomfortable when I've asked them what it is that they do to be the best version of themselves; they knew what they should be doing but they weren't creating the time to do it. Making that time and stopping and getting off the hamster wheel for a while to refocus and reframe should be a regular part of your life. I know it's hard, but empathy has to start with you.

Much of what I say in this chapter may seem obvious and come naturally to you. If so, then you're one of the lucky few if you are looking after "I" in every area. Even if you are, what you maybe need to ask is: am I teaching my team to do the same? Am I not only leading by example but also sharing what is giving me such a rewarding routine?

Why is it that when we hear of top sports professionals using techniques such as goal-setting, visualisation techniques, mantras, mind exercises and, of course, fitness routines that we accept that as the way they get to the peak of their game. Yet few team leaders, let alone team members in the business world, are either taught or practise such techniques regularly. Often they are frowned on as a bit flaky and unnecessary, yet they are every bit as effective outside the sports world as in.

Michael Phelps apparently set his goals at the age of eight. Winning an Olympic gold medal was at the top of the list, with a series of smaller goals leading up to that point. Wayne Rooney says he's used visualisation techniques since a young age and told ESPN[6]: "Part of my preparation is I go and ask the kit man what colour we're wearing – if it's red top, white shorts, white socks or black socks. Then I lie in bed the night before the game and visualise myself scoring goals or doing well. You're trying to put yourself in that moment and trying to prepare yourself, to have a 'memory' before the game." Emma Radicanu, who sensationally won the US Open at 18, says she has always been brought up to have huge mental strength

---

[6] Jamie Jackson, (2012), "Wayne Rooney reveals visualisation forms important part of preparation", The Guardian, 17 May, available at: https://www.theguardian.com/football/2012/may/17/wayne-rooney-visualisation-preparation

alongside her physical training. Days before winning she said she would fall asleep visualising walking up with her team to collect the trophy after winning.

Daily routines

Some leaders I spoke to did have exceptionally structured and enviable daily routines. Louise Dell, who runs Kyero.com, a fantastic business that helps you find your dream property overseas, starts her days with meditation at 5:30am seven days a week, followed by yoga or strength training in the gym. She told me it's crucial to her that she "gets the day right" before starting work.

That doesn't mean we all have to start our day at 5:30am, follow *The Miracle Morning*[7] routine (a great, but not to be taken too literally, book by Hal Elrod) or be the next Mark Wahlberg, who hit social media headlines a few years ago for his extreme daily routine (see diagram).

---

[7] *Hal Elrod, (2017), The Miracle Morning, John Murray Learning, First ed*

Time	Activity	
2:30am	**Wake up**	✓
2:45am	**Prayer time**	✓
3:15am	**BREAKFAST #1:** *Steel oats, peanut butter, blueberries and eggs*	✓
3:40–5:15am	**WORKOUT #1**	✓
5:30am	**BREAKFAST #2:** *Protein shake, 3 turkey burgers, 5 pieces of sweet potato*	✓
6am	**Shower**	✓
7:30am	**Golf**	✓
8am	**SNACK:** *10 Turkey meatballs*	✓
9:30am	**Cryo chamber recovery**	✓
10:30am	**BREAKFAST #3:** *Grilled chicken salad with 2 hard-boiled eggs,* *olives, avocado, cucumber, tomato and lettuce*	✓
11am	**Family time/meetings/work calls**	
1pm	**LUNCH:** *New york steak with green peppers*	
2pm	**Meetings/work calls**	
3pm	**Pick up kids from school**	
3:30pm	**SNACK:** *Grilled chicken with bok choy*	
4pm	**WORKOUT #2**	
5pm	**Shower**	
5:30pm	**DINNER/FAMILY TIME:** *Fish (halibut or cod or sea bass) with veggies* *(such as sautéed spinach and bok choy)*	
7:30pm	**Bedtime**	

We've all seen people follow extreme routines to the letter only to switch to another fad routine or diet when it becomes apparent that sustaining them impacts their lives far more negatively than expected.

None of these routines should be taken literally. Whilst they might claim short-term mental and physical gains, most of us can't or wouldn't want to go to the extremes of Mark Wahlberg.

In fact, even the legendary Wahlberg revealed in a recent interview that during the lockdown his wake up time was closer to 9am - and he didn't hit the gym until 10:30am. So he really is human!

Personally I'm nowhere near as structured as Louise Dell of Kyero, who has clearly found a daily routine that's worked for her for many years. However, starting the day in the right frame of mind is probably one of the single most simple and most important lessons we can learn. It's not easy and it takes stopping for a few minutes before jumping into the day, something many of us find hard to make time for. Sometimes I fail at it, but I do make a conscious effort to start the day happy and focused as often as possible. I keep practising it and, little by little, the habit builds. It's too easy to rush into the day and get swallowed by minor issues and distractions that really shouldn't be allowed our attention. It's even easier when working from home or on a non-office day when your commute is nonexistent!

Chapter 3

Find your routine

The more you read, the more you learn, the more you experiment, the closer you come to finding a routine or activity that works best for you. For example, I find meditating first thing in the morning makes my chimp brain (more on this in Chapter 5) shout and scream at me that I may as well have stayed in bed. Meditation is a fantastic and much-needed skill in such a noisy world but it simply doesn't work for me first thing. But if I end my working day with just 15 minutes of sitting still and trying to think about absolutely nothing at all, I know I come away calmer, stronger and relaxed.

We'll hear more about the chimp or rather the A.P.E. Brain® from Dr. Jon Finn of Tougher Minds later in the book. The A.P.E. is the emotional limbic part of your brain that is there to protect you from danger with its quick fight-or-flight mechanism, but it also causes us to worry and crave quick rewards, and generally leads us astray if we don't learn to balance and condition it via practising good habits through our logical frontal brain.

No matter how well trained our A.P.E. is, finding the balance between the draw of building the best team, achieving great work together and leading (as well as making sure you devote enough time to your health and happiness to keep you sane) is a challenge we may never perfect.

Chapter 3

My brain is definitely most active and useful in the first few hours after waking up, so I tend to write down my aims for the day, highlight any potential challenges then tackle the work-related tasks that take the most brain power first thing. Then just as the lull sets in I go for a run or a walk; once the serotonin and feel-good hormones kick in, I can return for stage two.

If I don't make time for that run or walk, I know my day will quickly deteriorate. The chimp often tries to talk me out of it (and sometimes beats me), but it's an argument I've become much better at winning.

Lessons from leaders

Kiran Haslam, of Princess Yachts, struck a chord when he told me: "I think an active life is a beautiful one." His 'meditation' is doing something active that challenges the brain, takes physical effort and gives him a sense of purpose and achievement.

When I last spoke to him he'd just spent six weeks following the guidance of YouTube videos and building a garage for his cars. He's a massive film and music fan, a celebrated jazz musician, a petrol-head (and in his last role helped revive the brand and fortunes of Bentley cars) and a proud and devoted husband and Dad. He finds keeping active and having a wide range of interests that are NOT all work related the best way for him to stay on track.

I often hear Kiran's voice in my head when I've been stuck at my desk or been sucked back onto the hamster wheel for too long.

Taking time to do something constructive, indulge a passion or develop even a tiny bit more of a new skill all give my brain that essential boost to keep on track. It made me even more aware of how our words can impact those around us far more than we maybe expect.

Find your passion

If I feel better for the constant reminders and a few well-placed comments to look after me (from someone like Kiran) then my team and all those around me can surely benefit in the same way. You're not telling your team how to live, you're not preaching, nor are you boasting. You're sharing and leaving people to decide what works best for them. As was the case with Kiran's comments to me, it's sometimes the smallest of comments that can surprise you with just how much impact they have.

When I spoke to Bruce Tip Poon, the founder of G Adventures, one of the world's largest independently-owned adventure travel companies, he told me he used to cover 300,000 miles a year before Covid-19 hit. Even with all that flying time he set a goal to do some kind of physical activity every day. One day it might be running; the next, yoga or even just a walk.

The goal, the mindset and having things you love outside work are key, he told me. For Bruce, those include watching sports games, theatre and he has a keen interest in art. He believes that these distractions contribute to him doing his best work.

Inspiration

Bruce believes that being the best version of himself enables him to have that empathy and then to inspire each individual in his team to be the best they can be: *"I'm a big believer that people shouldn't work all the time. I encourage this within my organisation. In order for you to do your best work you have to be inspired outside of work. I don't believe in long hours. If people work every day until 10pm, and all they do is work, work, work, they can only regurgitate what they know.*

"My most valuable people are people that can tell me what they don't know. Just as the best ideas aren't known yet, to you or your people, the most valuable people in your organisation are people that constantly deliver what they don't know, bringing new ideas all the time. The people who just regurgitate the same values, the same business because they work all the time, become very, very ineffective very quickly because they work too much.

"I encourage my people to find beautiful things they're passionate about outside of work (art, architecture, food, wine, travel, collecting stamps, antique shows). Whatever it is that they find becomes equally important to me, because it helps them feel happy and do their best work while at work."

We know we need to be careful that work doesn't take over our lives entirely. We genuinely cannot be at our best if we don't focus on our health and give our brains an opportunity to regularly recharge. Your brain simply isn't designed to be at its peak for more than a few hours a day. It needs to recharge. Yet many of us neglect our brains even if we are excellent at looking after our physical fitness.

Clear boundaries

Our brains, just like our bodies, need exercise and rest. As simple and obvious as it may sound, it will actually be harder than ever to look after our brains and bodies in a less structured and more hybrid environment. Without the clear boundary between work and home, the forced breaks provided by commuting and the natural distractions from work, such as colleagues stopping by your desk for a chat, it is too easy to just keep going. Add in the noise of all the extra communication tools we depend on to work in the hybrid world (more on the distractions we face in Chapter 6), plus the added distractions around us and our teams at home, and a refocus on how we structure our lives is essential.

We need to establish a clear divide between work and personal life, or be very clever at managing the blurred lines between them. We know an overworked team won't produce their best results, so why would we believe that as leaders we are any different?

Chapter 3

Keeping the Balance

Two of the key components of emotional intelligence that underpin the ability to lead with empathy are self-awareness and self-regulation. Being self-aware gives us an understanding of our own strengths, weaknesses, skills and abilities and helps us focus on where we need to improve and learn, together with where we have most to give. It is the basis of self esteem and confidence; without it we can't begin to understand or help others grow and learn.

Self-regulation is our ability to manage our emotions, desires and behaviours in order to be the best version of ourselves and, in turn, be great leaders and role models.

We know that when we eat well, sleep well, exercise efficiently and take regular breaks that we are generally more calm, productive, innovative, self-aware and able to self-regulate.

What happens when we lose balance?

When we lose focus and stop looking after ourselves mentally, physically and emotionally, we become more stressed, less productive, find it harder to make good decisions and ultimately become ineffective team leaders. Empathy and understanding require calm thought and a considered approach. They do not come easily to a frazzled or overworked brain.

But if we're fully aware of this fact, why do so many of us frequently fail at working on ourselves, the "I" in teams?

The majority of leaders I've spoken to over the past year say they are working even longer hours, taking fewer breaks, booking back-to-back meetings on Zoom and pushing their 'me' time further and further into the future. Even the chance to catch a breath between meetings when you sit on a train or have a coffee has been replaced with a quick change from one face to the next on your screen (usually with only seconds to spare).

How many great leaders, previous bosses, role models or friends have you admired and looked up to in the past who you know are stressed, tired, unfit, constantly chasing their tails and never there for their family, friends or hobbies?

Hopefully the answer is none.

Living the dream whilst working the extreme?

Occasionally we may admire someone who seems to be living the dream whilst working at full tilt. However, behind the scenes they turn out to be either fantastic self-publicists or just around the corner from burnout. Working to extremes and remaining fit, happy and healthy is almost impossible. There has to be balance.

It would be easy to blame the forced conditions of lockdowns for the further blurring of lines between work and personal life. When you're out with friends, watching a show or skiing down a mountain it's much easier to want to put aside your work for the day. But we know that lockdowns alone are not to blame. As a nation, work has been creeping further and further into our downtime for many years. We're surrounded by devices and platforms that lure us back in. Making sure we separate our time between work, family, friends and leisure is now harder but more essential than ever before.

Leading by example

If I ate burgers for breakfast, rarely exercised and spent meetings yawning and trying to prop my eyes open, why would my team listen to me when I say it's so important to look after themselves? Now I know they wouldn't have to see my breakfast, but they would have to suffer my yawns. As leaders we have to master the skill, refine the habit and make it happen! It's then the smallest of comments or actions that might be all that's needed to inspire others to keep the balance too.

If I go out for a walk at a random time in the day because my head is buzzing, it's because I can work better after that 20-minute refresh. Showing others you do something as simple as this is hopefully sowing this seed in people's brains so they update how they think about their working day. Maybe lunchtime doesn't have to be one hour at a set time. Maybe they can go for a walk, take the dog out or go to the gym as long as their work is completed within the framework we've agreed as a team.

Dangers of ignoring our needs

A huge amount of business owners and team leaders I speak to, however, are denying themselves the basics of health, working smarter or reclaiming more time for themselves to recharge and stay in peak mental health due to the overwhelming workloads they have succumbed to. The dangers of this are clear and if we don't readdress the basics now, how can we possibly expect our teams to do it and perform at peak levels?

We have to remember that knowledge is only potential power; it is putting the knowledge into practice that creates a positive impact.

The new normal

If the new way of working has derailed your routine, even in small ways, then consider what it's probably done to your team. Some may have learnt great new skills and be entrenched in new routines, but maybe some of these routines are not healthy, and certainly not good for business if you want the best performing and happiest team there can be.

If you're lucky enough to consistently maintain a perfect balance then share this next section with your team or a colleague who needs it.

My story

Two years ago I personally had the pleasure of a week on a ward in King's College Hospital. What was supposed to be a routine GP check-up turned into: *"Just wait a minute, Mr McMahon, I need to check something."*

When the GP returned he calmly told me he'd called an ambulance as I was having a heart attack. *"No, I'm not,"* I said. *"I feel fine. I ran five miles yesterday. I'm fit and healthy."* He went on to explain that I may be right, but if I wasn't having a heart attack I soon would be.

Whilst waiting for the ambulance to arrive I told him that he was mistaken and asked if he could at least let me drive home to pick up my wife. *"But you're having a heart attack, John,"* he said. I maintained my stance: *"No, I'm not."*

My first overnight stay in hospital wasn't calming in any way. A prisoner, handcuffed to two guards, was chained to the bed next to me. Then it was discovered that the bloke at the far end of the ward had a bottle of vodka hidden in his bag (now empty – it was doing an amazing job of reacting with whatever medication he'd been given).

The sound of emergency alarms, ongoing panic and three security guards sitting on a patient to quiet him were replaced by the constant beeping of my heart monitor. The monitor, clearly now in overdrive, was telling everyone I was about to have that heart attack!

Following a week of tests and head scratching I was proved right. I had not had a heart attack; what had been detected was an electrical block that mimicked a heart attack. I would need more tests, but I'd be fine. I was discharged. However, there was no denying that running two businesses and leaving little downtime had contributed to my health scare.

It's amazing how a week like that forces you to reprioritise. There is a lot of time to think, and a lot of time to make solemn promises to 'whatever being you may believe in'. For me it was promises of more 'me' time, less work, less worry, more time for family, friends and fun: a decent work-life balance.

The wake up call

When I started to openly share my heart attack scare it quickly became apparent that I was not alone.

"I don't want to hear the words 'charged to 100' ever again in my life," one leader told me. He promised himself he'd take more time out since his heart scare last year. Sadly, he told me he has yet to find time.

Chapter 4

Earlier this year a post on LinkedIn went viral: *So I Had A Heart Attack.*[8] It was shared from a hospital bed by Jonathan Frostick who had realised (almost too late) that his working life was spilling over into what, pre-pandemic, had once been personal time. His promise to himself when he left the hospital was going to be: *"I'm not spending all day on Zoom anymore."*

When you love what you do

Isn't it amazing how quickly we can lose the work-life balance? I love my work, as I'm guessing you do, but it's easy to slip back to unhealthy levels. Richard Branson once said on his Virgin.com blog[9]: *"I've never really understood why so many people separate work and play; it's all living."* As one of the most empathetic leaders ever, his meaning behind the words was that you need to make your work life fun and exciting, so it's more like life, not the other way around.

He went on to say: *"It's amazing what we can achieve and the fun we can have when we're all on the same team."* But if you're not diligent in your routines and in looking after YOU, then your effectiveness as a person (let alone as a leader) can never be at its best.

---

[8] *https://www.linkedin.com/posts/jonathanfrostick_heartattack-hsbc-decisionmaking-activity-6787207960864014336-auZR/*

[9] *Gael Cooper, (2018), "Richard Branson Thinks You're Organizing Your Work Life AllWrong. Here's How He Does It", Inc.com, 12 April*

Free rein to experiment

I've tried to give people free rein to experiment with many types of leadership styles in my businesses over the years. I've sometimes been led into the belief that a more hardened, traditional, almost autocratic approach is what's needed, but it has always failed to bring out the best in people or business. In addition to making us great as a team, I've found that leading with empathy has proved to be the most rewarding and enjoyable. Having a happy and engaged team who genuinely love their jobs and want to improve every day is one of the best feelings I have ever experienced in my working life.

An empathetic leader cannot afford to be overly stressed or burnt out. You need to be the best version of yourself, and that means starting with you and leading from the front. Before we dive into how best to do that, let's understand why we're not already our best selves!

When we have an understanding of the mechanics of the mind everything becomes much clearer. I'm fascinated by what makes people tick. You'll soon see why.

Train Your Brain; Teach Your Team

My interest in the complexities of the brain and how we can become better people, better leaders and better at building a great team culture by learning how to be more productive and focused on the positives has been a passion for many years. The fact that we are lucky enough to be born in a prosperous part of the world and can do anything we fully set our minds to is fascinating.

Legends such as Napoleon Hill who wrote *Think and Grow Rich*[10] back in 1937 inspired me to aim to continuously learn and improve, and to try to then share what I learnt with those around me. Rich in Hill's context doesn't mean selfish riches by the way. Rich means a high quality of life and what we make of ourselves and those around us, just as much as it relates to money. The book says anyone can do anything they set their mind to; don't whinge and say you can't. Set your mind to your goals and you will find a way.

---

[10] *Napoleon Hill, (1937), Think And Grow Rich, Tarcher Perigree*

Brain training

I've read many books on the subject of how our brains can either be taught to lead and inspire us to great things and great lives or trick you into thinking everyone else around you is far better and more competent than you. I highly recommend reading *The Chimp Paradox*[11] by Prof Steve Peters and *The Power Of Habit*[12] by Charles Duhigg for instance. These and others like them are great at explaining why we need to pay more attention to training and focusing our brains, but few explain exactly how to do this in simple terms or, just as importantly, how to then help our teams and those around us to be able to do the same.

Teaching those around you how they can have less stress, less chaos, less self doubt and excel at everything they put their minds to is a skill that surely has to be at the heart of every leader's skill set? Teaching yourself all the skills that lead to optimum productivity and satisfaction is one thing, but sharing those with an entire team multiplies the benefits across an entire organisation.

My challenge has always been how to teach personal growth and development in a way that doesn't preach, isn't overly scientific, is easy to follow and, the big one, in a way that doesn't claim that you are the expert and undisputed authority on the subject. As I learn, I want to share; as I make mistakes and fall off the self improvement wagon, I don't want to have to hide it.

---

[11] *Prof Steve Peters, (2012), The Chimp Paradox, Vermilion*

[12] *Charles Duhigg, (2013), The Power of Habit, Random House Books*

Chapter 5

Training the brain is a slow and constant journey and isn't a skill that, once learnt, automatically stays with you. Stop following a healthy diet and you will probably put on weight; stop training your brain daily and you'll very quickly lose the skills you've learnt.

When I originally heard Dr Jon Finn, who you were introduced to in Chapter 2, give a talk, I thought I had been practising most of what he was suggesting for years: stay fit, eat well, sleep well, set goals, reflect at the end of each day, be productive, encourage my team to do the same.

The problem is that the busier you get, the more challenges come your way. The faster your pace of life, the more distractions you face, and the easier it is to fall out of good habits. Work can overtake life, and, whilst working long hours and constantly being 'switched on' may have become the norm, it's actually counterproductive. The brain needs looking after to be at its best and crucially at its productive and efficient best.

We've always been taught that we need to exercise, eat healthily and get good sleep to protect our hearts, stay fit, look good and feel good. Rarely, however, do we stop and think about our brains. However, everything we do is powered by our brain so why aren't we taught to look after it in just the same way?

Looking after our brain requires a good combination of diet, sleep and exercise, alongside an awareness of how our brain state changes throughout the day, what it needs and how it can be recharged by building a series of tiny habits.

Chief Habit Mechanic™

I decided to go back to school and learn from the professionals in Dr Jon Finn's team and have recently graduated with the Tougher Minds *Chief Habit Mechanic Leadership Certificate*[13] (a course I undertook over a six-month period that I now try to teach to the team on a weekly basis).

It's a simple yet hugely effective format. As a result, my own personal productivity is possibly the best it's ever been. My focus is almost always on positives rather than dwelling on negatives and challenges out of my control. On the days where the negatives all come along at once (as seems to happen in life!), I now have proven techniques to put them into context and deal with them without getting totally derailed.

These were skills I had practised for many years, very often with a good degree of success, but now the consistency is much easier to maintain. The fact that they are backed by science also gives me the confidence to keep them up daily and, most importantly, share them with the team. They are skills that I can gradually teach the team without expecting raised eyebrows or a, "Here we go again, John's on another happiness crusade!"

Learning and letting your team learn the basic facts and techniques in a course such as this is an essential part of training them to adapt to the non 9 to 5 world. We can't expect everyone to adapt, form their own routines, look after

---

[13] *https://www.tougherminds.co.uk/chief-habit-mechanic-leadership-certificate/*

their mental health and be a great member of a team without any training in just how we can do this.

What we know versus what we do

Most of us know that we need to eat more fruit and veg each day. We're familiar with the concept of walking 10,000 steps and not overeating or drinking too much alcohol. Most of us don't put that knowledge into practice consistently every single day. Why is that?

I don't have three degrees or a PhD in the science of the brain so, although I have the certification, I've asked Dr Jon Finn (Tougher Minds) to explain: *"Our brain doesn't run on knowledge; it runs on habits. Leadership training in the past hasn't considered that. It doesn't actually consider what is going on inside the brain of a leader.*

"In the new non 9 to 5 working environment you describe in this book we're going to need to become even better at solving problems and to make it really easy for our teams to be good at communication and collaboration. Because that's how we get good at solving problems, by working together.

"That means that a leader's new number one priority is to help the brains of their team members work really well. In particular the prefrontal cortex. This new priority means that the traditional ways we have thought about leadership are dead; they don't work anymore.

"As you mentioned earlier, the metaphor that I think is most powerful in the modern world is that everyone in your team has got their own snowmobile, and they are moving up a mountain, collectively. The conditions on the mountain are changing all the time. The top of the mountain is your goal, your objectives. It's our job now as leaders to help every individual get really good at using their snowmobile in these challenging conditions. Connected to that, we've got to be the person who helps the team to communicate and collaborate in these challenging conditions. It's all about building good habits and helping those around us to build good habits."

Autopilot takes over

Dr Jon likes to share the following scrambled sentence to make his point:

To make sense of words it deosn't mttaer in what order the ltteers in a wrod are, the olny ipmoetnt tihng is taht the frist and lsat ltteer are in the rghit pclae.

It's clear that without too much mental exertion you can read those jumbled up words. Why? Because what we do most of the time is mindless. We are running on autopilot, habits. Some of those habits will enhance our individual or leadership performance; some are extremely unhelpful.

I've learnt from Dr Jon Finn that habits are energy efficient because we don't exert energy thinking and making decisions. We have evolved to save energy.

Dr Jon went on to explain that: "*For most of our existence energy (food) has been a very scarce resource. Thinking consciously burns a lot of energy (your brain uses around 25% of your total energy output). Habits make thinking and doing things more energy efficient. So we have evolved to run on habits.*

"*This means we do not think about most of the things we do. This includes breathing. We just do it. We do not talk ourselves through the process e.g., 'breathe in, breathe out'. The way you are reading this book is largely habit. It is a very automated process. The way we make a decision about someone we have just met for the first time happens in about five seconds. We are not deliberately being judgemental or critical: it's just the way our brain works.*

"*Habits become more dominant and powerful with practice. Science shows that when we repeat or practice a certain aspect of behaviour (thought or action), we hardwire it into our brains via a process known as neuroplasticity. This means that the 100 billion or so neurons in your brain are like plasticine. Your neurons grow, reshape and die depending on what you practice.*

"*Our habits dominate what we do and how we think. My experience of the world is what I am in the habit of paying attention to, and the same goes for all of us. If I pay attention to my failures in life and the setbacks I've experienced, that becomes my reality. If I pay attention to how fantastic I am, and how nothing is ever my fault, that becomes my reality.*

Chapter 5

"Our family, friends, colleagues, teams and organisations all run on habits. The habits that are most dominant are those that they practice the most."

The operating system

Part of our brain, the limbic system, largely houses our habits. It has three main remits:

- Survival
- Our social status: how we're perceived by important people
- Saving energy

Dr Jon calls this Alive Perceived Energy: the A.P.E.™ brain I mentioned in Chapter 3. We can think of this as the place our autopilot habits are formed and developed - influenced by our fight-or-flight mechanisms. Many of our habits like this are invisible and, over time, become hardwired into how we think. The more we practise, the better we get at doing something. For example, to get really good at worrying or criticising yourself all you need to do is practise it! You'll soon be an expert.

These types of habits, he tells us, are the biggest waste of resources for any individual in any 24 hour period. They're invisible; we don't really see ourselves doing them, yet we're all carrying them around. These autopilot habits are often competing against the type of things that we're trying to do to be healthy, happy and at our best. It's not just an individual problem because if they're the biggest waste of resources for an individual, they're also the biggest waste of resources for a team, a family unit or an organisation.

We've built on shaky ground

Dr Jon Finn summed it up perfectly: *"It's not our fault. We've been educated in the wrong way. We've been told that if you give yourself or your people more knowledge, that will help them to overcome the stress problem or that more knowledge will help you lead your team to be better. But it won't because these are all habit problems. So, to overcome the problems, we have to help our people to build better habits, to move from the knowing to the doing to the habit."*

Without going into too much technical detail the good news is that there is another part of our brain that can help us and our team to analyse and break these habits: the prefrontal cortex. In Tougher Minds language it's called the H.A.C.™ (Helpful Attention Control) brain and is home to our willpower; we can use this to unpick one unhealthy habit at a time and replace it with a positive one. In other words, we can manage the A.P.E.™!

Through this process we can strengthen the parts of our brain that help us perform at our best and make it easier for us to become outstanding leaders, and, in turn, to help nurture outstanding teams.

Dr Jon suggests that as empathetic leaders we need to adjust our own settings and become Habit Mechanics™ , and then, since we lead from the front, encourage our team members to do the same.

Chapter 5

This simple concept of building gradual habits and focusing on things that we may take for granted, such as diet, sleep and exercise, make this a powerful foundation when it comes to leading your team in a non-traditional working environment.

One observation that Dr Jon taught me around the A.P.E.™ brain that will be particularly important for you and your team to learn as you all adapt to less structured working environments is the need to manage distraction. We are all surrounded by distractions and our A.P.E.™ brain loves distractions.

It's easy to say we must overcome all this noise, but what are the real distractions and how do we overcome them so that productivity and customer satisfaction remain at their optimum?

We're Surrounded by Distractions

I have a love-hate relationship with social media. Having run a digital marketing agency for over 20 years, I love the endless potential of the platforms to deliver your brand message or product to exactly the right people with laser precision. It's sometimes easy to forget just what a rapid change there has been since the internet first launched and the tsunami of social media swept into our lives.

As incredible as these social platforms, instant news updates and always-on messaging applications are, we now need to be acutely aware of how quickly the balance can tip. We need to prevent them from taking over our lives. We also need to make sure they don't take over our teams.

Digital noise

Leading with empathy means understanding how much that noise can affect you and your team in their ability to be at their best. The pressure to reply to emails and messages instantly, perform as well as those carefully crafted celebrities and business leaders on social platforms, have the same fun as our friends seem to be having in their carefully edited photos, as well as digesting the bombardment of news stories that can leave even the most resilient in a state of constant concern, is huge.

When I first started MCM I had to explain to people what a website was and why they needed one. Google hadn't launched and social media was unheard of, so to reach our potential audience we had to use more traditional means.

My first gem of an idea involved targeting 1,000 businesses within a 20-mile radius to try to sell them a website. Today I could have an ad set up in minutes and not only target the precise location but also job title, industry, income and a whole host of focused data. Back then I had to buy a list of names and addresses (very few had an email address) and send a letter or brochure that nine in ten recipients may never open nor have an interest in. There was also no way of knowing if those letters had been opened.

Lessons in marketing

I decided a letter was boring so I had 1,000 postcards created with the slogan: *"Don't be afraid of the web, get on it with MCM Net."* I then managed to source a toy factory that would supply me with 1,000 halloween spiders and webs, and we bought 1,000 flat-packed pizza boxes.

My wife Theresa (who has the patience of the Saint of the same name) and I spent the next week assembling the boxes whilst carefully stretching the cotton wool web on the inside, popping the postcard on top and positioning a large plastic black spider above it. Each of these boxes then had to have a label carefully printed and stuck on the outside, and a set of stamps licked and stuck on the top corner!

We trundled to the post office with batches of pizza boxes and drew our fair share of questioning looks. After all that I sat by the phone and waited for the flood of phone calls. We had three.

The first two were from personal assistants (PAs), both of whom said they were of a nervous disposition and nearly had a heart attack when they opened the box (and threatened legal action). The third was a local business that absolutely loved the gall of what we'd come up with and signed up for a website the very next day. It wasn't quite the success I had imagined, but not a total failure. It had been a huge amount of effort, and not particularly sustainable.

Empathy with your audience!

I hadn't factored in the fact that many of the recipients would have PAs and secretaries and probably wouldn't open the box themselves. This taught me a huge lesson in the need to understand your audience and properly imagine yourself in their shoes. Now, thankfully, we're much more likely to send sweets or chocolates than spiders and it's a story I've told team members many times so they don't make the same mistake as me. Always try to think how others might think: that not only makes you human and empathetic, but in our business identifying exactly who the audience are and how they might feel is the key to a great deal of the success we've had with client campaigns.

Today when we target a social account with carefully placed ads we can be fairly sure they will reach the intended recipient. Even email marketing is still very effective. Why? Because we're all chained to our laptops and phones 24/7. We're surrounded by platforms, messages, devices and electronic noise.

Breathing space

When I first started working we received a stack of mail each day. When you opened that mail you knew you wouldn't have to do the task again until the following day. You had time to breathe and act on what had come in and what else you had to do. Today, no matter how quickly you empty your email inbox, it refills every minute.

The potential for our minds to be drawn back to work by email and social media without us realising it is there every minute. In fact, research by Dr David Ellis at Lancaster University for a House of Commons study on the impact of screen use demonstrated that people have little insight regarding how many times they check their phone each day.

How screen time haunts us

Measuring screen time directly, Dr Ellis' team found that people were checking their smartphone an amazing 85 times a day on average, both consciously and unconsciously. Another report[14] from the US from early 2021 showed nearly half those surveyed spent between five and six hours per day on their phones, not including work-related use.

Even if each time you pick up your phone it's just a quick look at the news or the weather, that interruption quickly adds up and eats into productivity. Most recorded sessions on phones are less than two minutes long, but can easily start a chain reaction. Half of sessions started within three minutes of the previous one: read an email, click a link, end up on LinkedIn or Google and very quickly we've broken our focus (and studies[15] show that it then takes an average of 23 minutes to get back to deep focus again). Teaching ourselves to turn the phone off, leave it in another room or at least put it out of reach is proven to hugely increase focus and productivity. Encouraging your team to do the same multiplies that productivity exponentially.

When I was sending spiders in boxes to promote our services, people opened the mail, skim read it, filed around 90 per cent of it in the bin, and then acted on the 10 per cent that warranted attention. Then you'd get on with your day.

---

[14] *Statista, (2021), 'How much time on average do you spend on your phone on a daily basis?', 21 February,*

[15] *Daniela Gudith, Ulrich Klocke and Gloria Mark, (2008) "The Cost of Interrupted Work: More Speed and Stress", University of California Irvine*

You didn't click a link and you didn't Google something that caught your eye in that letter, nor did you then see an alert on your LinkedIn account that reminded you to reply to an email (where your reply was then instantly replied to).

Today we are surrounded by electronic distractions and these are often so intertwined with our work life that it's easy to find an article or a post that prompts a thought, an idea or a reminder that then draws you back to email or sends your brain into overdrive. It's far harder to progress your day.

The consequences of distraction

Working in a hybrid world means we're likely to be surrounded by these distractions even more. There's more need for communication channels to replicate the office interactions for your team, and there are fewer natural breaks for journeys, lunch or face-to-face conversations to create those natural divisions of time.

Being constantly distracted means less productivity and more stress, less focus and more rabbit holes to fall down. Not only will this lead to being a less effective leader but if we don't recognise how it can affect our daily life then we won't be able to help our teams avoid the same traps.

For people like us who love our jobs, it's become much easier to work than not work. It's easier to slip back in front of the laptop or phone to clear out that email inbox than finally learn how to play that guitar. We're busy, and the rest of life can wait.

Inbox zero may be a fantastic feeling, but you know that within hours it will be full again. We become less effective with a great deal of the work we allow ourselves to get pulled back in by; it is far more efficient to stop, take a break and return to it in good time.

How do we manage distraction?

Part of our brain is constantly looking for a quick fix, be that leisure or work. Even just jumping to check some emails when a report you're writing gets too tough can give the brain that quick hit and soon derail us. If we can learn this basic concept and how to get better at managing our days, our brains (and those of our teams) will become far more efficient.

In the last chapter, Dr Jon Finn of Tougher Minds introduced us to the concept of our A.P.E. brain. Another concept he talks about in his courses is H.U.E., which stands for Horribly Unhelpful Emotions. He encourages his course participants to imagine a character named Hue, who runs the A.P.E. brain.

Hue can make us think and do things that are not very helpful, such as watching Netflix or working late instead of recharging the brain through healthy habits. Hue is always scanning the horizon for threats or fun things to do that give instant rewards so needs help from Will (or Willemiena), who runs the Will Power (H.A.C.) section of our brain. Will Power doesn't come from being single-minded and simply denying ourselves nice things. Will Power helps Hue by building habits that enable *him* to survive and thrive.

Chapter 6

Journalling: the brain dump

I've never been a fan of the word journalling. It feels a little high brow or forced so I use the rather technical term 'brain dump'. Whatever you call it, it is a rather simple yet hugely effective tool to quieten and order the mind at the end of a day. No matter how well you manage your time and health, we live in an extremely fast paced world. Our brains fill with over 6,000 thoughts a day according to one study by Queen's University in Canada[16]; add that to your emails, meetings and the inevitable crises and fires that have a habit of starting when you least need them and it becomes hard to switch off.

The brain dump is such a simple and effective way to empty your mind and lead you to a place of clarity. Pen and paper is best for this as there seems to be an unconscious connection when your thoughts flow to the paper (and it's time away from a screen). At the end of each day develop the habit of taking everything out of your head and onto paper:

- Write down anything about your day that's weighing on your mind.
- Put a tick next to anything that is within your control to solve.
- Ask yourself just how life threatening any of the issues you can't control really are.

---

[16] *Anne Craig, (2020), "Discovery of 'thought worms' opens window to the mind", Queen's Gazette, 13 July*

Undoubtedly you'll have a few issues that do seem tough, but when you see them on paper the majority of the problems that were buzzing inside your mind appear far less problematic, and writing them down brings perspective and clarity.

The very act of doing this calms your mind and helps you clearly see the bigger picture. When you revisit this list the next morning, or even days later, you'll wonder why on Earth you were worried (because many of the issues never materialised or were easily dealt with).

Stop obsessing

Knowing the list is there also means you tend to stop circling around the same thoughts (remember what Dr Jon said about our thinking habits in Chapter 5) as they are safely out of your mind and stored for the next day (if you need them!). It is also proven to give you a much better night's sleep.

Anything still on the list that needs solving is generally much easier to solve as it has stopped becoming an instant threat and your logical prefrontal cortex is in control rather than your limbic A.P.E.

Journalling can also include writing down what you're grateful for and what went well during the day. We so often forget to be thankful as we swiftly move on to the next challenge. Habitually making yourself stop, think, then write these positive thoughts down every day can be hugely rewarding and enlightening. I find that starting my day by writing next to the list all the positive things that happened the day before and what I'm thankful for has enabled me to develop the habit of always focusing on the good things in life and it really helps to put the challenges in focus. In fact, we now do this at our full team stand ups. Everyone tells us what they are currently most proud of in their working and personal life. It was awkward at first but the more we did it, the more natural it became. I'd really recommend it: not only does it help your team focus on the good but it also gives me a real buzz when I see happy smiling faces from people realising that actually life is pretty great!

We can start by changing one habit at a time until eventually we have weakened the unhelpful habits and empowered the positive ones that help us and our team to function at the highest level. One of the most powerful ways to do this is to have a clear direction and focus as to where you want to go. Most businesses have a mission statement and clear goals, but how often do we have this for our personal lives (the ones we're about to reclaim!)?

Creating a Plan and Setting Goals

We know that successful companies create a business plan, check that plan regularly, track progress and make adjustments where necessary. They hold themselves accountable and routinely seek outside help and advice. Yet how many of us create and diligently follow a 'life' plan? If we know the theory works for the most successful of businesses then why don't we all take time to create a personal plan?

Largely it's because we were never taught this skill at school. We feel it's not necessary and should be obvious. Life just happens and we go along with it. In a world that has more noise and less structure than ever, I hope personal planning will soon be firmly on every school syllabus.

Personal fulfilment

I can plot the most amazing, exciting and successful personal and business years I've had on a graph (I really love a spreadsheet!); these have always been years where I planned both work and life and got the balance as close to perfect (for me) as possible. They weren't years when I had my feet up, but they were years where alongside work I was training for a marathon, writing my goals and intentions daily, checking I was tracking against them, travelling and exploring an amazing country, learning a new skill, planning more evenings or days out as a family or simply making sure that when the weekend came I had enough energy and willpower to enjoy it.

New skills

Taking that extra time to create a plan is something that is so easy to say you don't have time for! Checking yourself daily and inviting others to hold you accountable for sticking to your plans can actually be a huge challenge. Learning how to make sure your balance is one that makes your life both enjoyable and rewarding is one skill that is guaranteed to improve your ability to lead. As we discussed in Chapter 3, the only way for you to lead with empathy is to put yourself first and develop yourself.

When you're in control of your own life, are constantly learning new skills and feeling fulfilled in both work and non-work activities it makes you someone people want to learn from. It also makes you someone qualified enough to help others to learn to be their best version of themselves. Ultimately this leads to a far happier, far more contented and hugely more productive team.

As empathetic leaders we can support our team members to get to know their own minds; it's one of the best ways to create greatness!

Foundational principles

Teaching even the basic principles of personal and work goal-setting to your team is guaranteed to positively affect behaviour and performance; if each member of your team takes even a small amount of notice of you sharing this knowledge you can expect to see a stronger and even more productive culture emerge. It's also a fun team activity and a great reason for some team remote or face-to-face sessions.

At the core of many people's concerns around the new way of working is the need to focus even more on creating our own structure and finding balance without getting swamped by the distractions we covered in Chapter 6. A key part of YOUR job as a leader is to show them how they can do this.

The benefits of the 9 to 5 world included structure and routine. The dangers of not being in that structure, as we've already discussed, are assuming everyone can create and keep to their own self-defined routines, structures and plans. It becomes even more essential that each individual's personal goals are thought about and defined, as well as their work-related goals so that home does not become solely about work.

You wouldn't let a builder build you a house without an architect's plan: you'd expect drawings and specifications, timescales and costs. You and your team may know what the goal for the business is, but how can we relate that to your and your team's individual goals and aspirations?

Fulfilled living

If the two can be aligned and considered in relation to the new potential that working from anywhere gives us, not only do we live happier, more fulfilled lives, but we and our teams will develop structure and direction that ultimately gives us a hugely productive environment. Helping people learn how to define and manage their goals will not only help you understand them more, help them grow and follow a path where they are at their best for both work and play, but also build further trust and understanding across the team.

Without goals we miss opportunities

You may already have a clear set of goals and beliefs, but that would put you amongst only 3 per cent of the population (and only 1 per cent of people actually write them down). So it's highly likely that even if you do, many members of your team will have no defined goals. Not only does that mean they could be missing great opportunities in all areas of their lives, but it also potentially makes people harder to manage, less easy to teach and motivate and less able to support others in the team.

By instilling the benefits of personal and professional goals you will create a team eager to follow and learn, constantly inspired and hungry for results and progress.

Better performance

Studies show that goals that are specific and challenging (but not completely out of reach) lead to higher performance. If your goals are too easy then you won't make much of a change in how you live your life, but if they are too challenging or unbalanced in their focus you will likely become demotivated and give up easily.

Balanced goals need to focus on all areas of your and your team's lives. They are highly personal and relevant to each individual. Achievement means different things to each of us, and recognising this in yourself and your team is crucial to their success at keeping focused. This means not all the details of your goals or those of your team need to be shared in detail. It is sharing the knowledge of how to set goals, regular encouragement to revisit and adjust them and then a broad understanding of the direction people want to go that will make them invaluable.

Your sat nav only works if you tell it where to go

The concept is simple. If you don't know where you want to go, how will you get there? You can still adjust the route towards your goals as priorities change, but having a general vision of your ideal life and a plan of how you might achieve that helps you stay focused and maintain progress. They don't have to be billionaire or world-domination goals, but they are a great excuse to sit down, take stock, focus and feel in control of your life.

Mountain mayhem

Plus, remember the snowmobile analogy? Imagine the scene if you are driving the snowmobile (as the leader) on the mountain and others (your team members) are also headed that way, but nobody has the summit as their goal. It would be destined for disaster. Likewise, if one or two members had no goal they'd most likely get in the way of even the most determined. Without personal or professional goals there will be chaos.

If you haven't set goals before, or maybe haven't done so for a while, this could be the simplest single exercise you undertake to restore a sense of balance and control to your days. If you then share the concept with your team you soon have a pretty formidable force of committed individuals that know their purpose in every area of life. You also need to accept that some may decide their goals mean they follow a totally new path in life, but as we'll discuss in Chapter 10 that's not necessarily a bad thing.

Read one of the classics such as *Brian Tracy's Goals*[17] to fully get the best out of the exercise but goals, focus, purpose (whatever word you choose) help you identify a series of aims that you believe you can achieve or move towards.

---

[17] *Brian Tracy, (2010), Goals, Berrett-Koehler Publishers*

My core goals

I have had a written set of goals for more than 20 years. Their core hasn't changed much in all that time but some of the long-term goals have been adjusted as I've changed and as my priorities have changed. Whether it is for you or not, I know that I am the best version of myself when I follow my core goals and try to make small steps in the right direction every day. I aim to read them daily and write them out several times a week. They keep me grounded, focused, calm and in control, all of which I know puts me in a much better frame of mind to lead and empathise with the team.

Finding balance

If I feel the balance tipping then I write them every day and then at least once a year I take time to totally review them, maybe make a few small course changes and keep them fresh. I find the act of viewing them or spending a little bit more time writing them down therapeutic. It is not some beast of greedy monetary wants that hangs over me taunting me each day. They are my rules for life. They encourage me to question what I do and help me stay aligned to what I truly believe is the best version of my life.

The core of my goals has never changed. I have ten key areas and each of these is then broken down into small achievable chunks so I can measure progress. They broadly centre around:

1. Health and fitness (body and mind)
2. Family and relationships
3. Career ambitions
4. Learning and self development
5. Helping others and the environment we live in
6. Hobbies
7. Financial
8. Ultimate (far reaching)
9. Appreciate everything
10. Enjoy – if this was my last day, did I do my best to enjoy it?

The starting line

Health and fitness always comes first; for most people if this area isn't under control, the rest are unlikely to follow. This doesn't mean obsessive regimes and certainly isn't all about physical activity. It's an awareness and focus on the state of mind and body. I'm not aiming for perfection (my chimp says that's not for me), but when mind and body are in good working order everything else becomes much easier.

The journey rather than the destination

I've found training for a marathon more rewarding than crossing the finish line; it's the goal and progress that feeds my brain more than the medal at the end. It's also never about time (thankfully!) and as a leader of individuals it's essential to recognise that some people will set huge goals; others, small goals, and success in either means different things to different people. Goals only become dangerous when people set themselves up for failure or fall into the comparison trap. It's key for this to be a very individual and non-competitive exercise.

Three ways to energise your goals and stay motivated:

1. Write down your goals

You don't have to use my ten key areas above but feel free to steal them as a basis. Don't rush it. Do it when you feel relaxed, not stressed. Write down your goals, where you'd really like to see yourself, what you'd like to achieve, what your ultimate life would look like, no matter how quiet or extreme. This is you and your goals. What do you really want to do? You need to think long, medium and short term, in the next month, year and lifetime. Refine the list over a few weeks. Identify your big vision and work backwards to achieve it. Break the list down into smaller goals; run a marathon in two years might become run six miles by next month and keep building up.

The first time you do this it doesn't feel natural. These are truly personal feelings and aims. Some, like running that marathon, may be easier to achieve if you share the goal with friends. Others may stay truly personal to you forever. I write my goals using an electronic pen on a Microsoft Surface alongside relevant photos. They sync with my phone and iPad and this means, wherever I am, if I'm feeling derailed I can take a quick glance and remind myself how to keep on track.

2. Visualise

Imagine how you will feel when you accomplish your goals. Look at your starting point and set yourself a challenging but achievable deadline. Visualise not only accomplishing the goal but also how you will get there. Work out which obstacles may derail you, what knowledge you need and make a plan for each step along the way. Visualise what success looks like for each step and be happy with the small steps you take each day towards your goals! Make it feel real.

3. Mood board

Create a board with photos of the life you want to create; mine has photos of countries I want to visit, inspirational people (past and present) whom I admire (including my much missed Dad), inspirational agencies and companies to fuel me with ideas to make MCM even better, plus photos especially of family holidays and fun events that keep me grounded and remind me just how lucky I am and what I should appreciate and not take for granted, no matter how bad any day may seem at the time.

It doesn't matter how you work with your goals; just find a way to make the process enjoyable for you. I guarantee you won't regret setting goals or revisiting them as part of your daily habit!

We are privileged to be in a position to change how we go about our lives in some way; a lot of our quality of life is down to the mind and how we think. When you use a mood board to reinforce what you want to achieve or how you want to live your life every day, eventually it becomes your habit to go about creating it.

Running for clarity

In May this year the team at MCM took part in the 100 Miles in May challenge for mental health charity Mind[18]. At the start some employees were concerned they wouldn't be able to do anywhere near 100 miles in a month so we agreed we'd make it an average of 100 miles per person. Everyone submitted their miles anonymously to the head of our wellbeing team.

The ripple effect

It wasn't long, however, until those who were concerned started publicly announcing their miles. An extra walk a day, a cycle or a five-a-side game all contributed to the totals and people began to realise that adding a few extra miles really wasn't that hard at all. When it sounded like each person had to run 100 miles the challenge seemed huge, but when people realised they could still achieve their goal by doing things they enjoyed, the challenge became rewarding and achievable.

I personally love the freedom and the hugely calming influence running has on my life. I came late to running, having followed

---

[18] *https://www.mind.org.uk/*

my wife Theresa's excellent example when she first pushed herself to train for the London Marathon. I used to call her mad for putting in all those hours and knew I'd never achieve such a feat. Seeing her do it really inspired me though and, at the age of 40 and too embarrassed to be seen wobbling down the street, I started training in secret on a running machine in the garage. Soon I was hooked and it's now a part of my life I would seriously struggle without. But even if you don't get bitten by the bug, finding something that works for you in some way is key.

Hannah Poulton of the Marketing Centre told me: *"Running is the one thing where I genuinely don't have headspace to think about anything else. Because I find it so hard, that I've just got to keep focused on putting one foot in front of the other!"* Now that's honesty for you, but it just shows you don't have to be superhuman or into extreme sports; anything that takes you away from a digital screen and gets your blood pumping for a while will support a better version of you.

We have even less of an excuse when it comes to diet. Again, how we choose to fuel our bodies doesn't have to be extreme or a total change, although Kiran at Princess Yachts highly recommends veganism. He admitted that his primary reason for being vegan is not the anti-animal-eating reason but how it makes him feel. It keeps him energetic and clear-minded, which, in turn, helps him to be a strong, empathetic leader.

Personal preference and choice

As before, the key is finding the combination and balance of productivity tools, brain calming techniques, exercise and diet that feels right for you and who you are. To lead with empathy you need to be the best version of yourself and you do need to be yourself. As Kiran told me: "*People who build an elaborate scaffold around themselves leave themselves wide open to being exposed. You need to be someone others can follow but you should never take yourself too seriously. Humour and humility are key skills to ensure you build trust with your team.*"

If you feel that time is tight and there's little time for goals, the next chapter is exactly what you and your team need.

Chapter 7

Reclaim Time and Productivity for You and Your Team

A key benefit of the flexible non 9 to 5 working life is being able to set our own routines. As a leader you can do your most challenging work at a time of day you know you're most productive. You will learn to recognise when you've hit a slump and need to recharge, and you can exercise at a time that suits you best or even find time to fit it in around the school run or morning jobs.

You have far more scope to schedule your best work when you know you will feel fully charged and schedule your meetings for a less productive time if they need less brain power.

In this chapter we look at some key strategies so you can find what works best for you and your team.

Start your day with intention

I've always loved to-do lists. From day one of starting the business in 1997 I used an A4 hardback notebook and every day I would start by writing the day and date at the top, carefully underline it and then start my list. I'd diligently carry over the items not achieved from the day before, add the new ones that had arrived since I started the list and try to put them in an order of priority. Then I'd diligently cross them off as the day went by.

It helped me focus, and I found it rewarding and inspiring to set my day up well.

The problem

The problem was I felt controlled by my own to-do list. My chimp would wake up and I'd feed him a few easy wins on the list. Over time I realised the big ones still needed to be tackled, and I'd wasted vital brain power.

Eat that frog

The book that changed my life was *Eat That Frog*[19] by Brian Tracy. He explains that making a list makes us 25 per cent more productive BUT it's how you act on that list that really lets you achieve this. He cites the Pareto rule that states 80 per cent of consequences come from 20 per cent of the causes. The rule can be applied to many areas and is a fascinating study in its own right, but as far as your tasks go roughly 20 per cent of them will achieve 80 per cent of your productivity for the day.

Brian suggests you write down everything you think you need to do and then focus on two or three items that you believe will bring the best results from the time available.

---

[19] *Brian Tracy, (2013), Eat That Frog, Hodder Paperback*

The primary task is likely to be one of the more difficult ones that you would normally have delayed in favour of the easy ones. That is your frog for the day. Eat it. You might not like it, but it probably won't taste as bad as you think and you will actually feel great afterwards.

The brilliant thing about eating those frogs each day is they stop sitting on your shoulder taunting you all day. You use your best brain power on them, you feel more relaxed and empowered when they are complete and you still have the fun of powering through the easier tasks that are left. Plus, even if you run out of time, you can trust the Pareto principle, which I have found to be true nearly every time. The 20 per cent you've just eaten in those couple of frogs has achieved 80 per cent of what will really matter in your day.

Realisation

As my agency grew and my to-do list grew longer, I found no matter how hard I focused on the frogs there were still a whole host of other things to do. Then, when I drew breath, I realised that we only had a finite amount of time in a working day and, in my opinion, the number one cause of stress and burnout is trying to do the impossible. We were not built to multitask.

A rolling list

Now I view the to-do list as a rolling list that does not have to be completed immediately. Some of the items are 'nice to do' or for 'one day in the future' so really those are a record of a bigger vision for the business. Some of those items might get deleted because they no longer seem important, but this list is just as effective as the brain dump we discussed in Chapter 6.

Structure

I now add everything that I really need to do to my calendar, including exercise, lunch and calls I need to make, both personal and business. Doing this makes me be totally realistic with what I can achieve well in a day and what is simply not possible. We really weren't built for multi-tasking. Anything from my list that doesn't make it into the calendar for the next day simply isn't important enough or can be done another day. I enter everything that is important into the calendar up to several weeks ahead. This often means I'm left with an empty list or a few items that get moved to the future list or that I can delegate.

Be the change

If, as leaders, we feel stressed our team will not find us approachable. If we are out of control, we are piling additional pressure onto our teams because there will inevitably be times where tight deadlines that we haven't managed well require people to work until midnight. This is exactly what we want to avoid; we need to set the example. If we're asking people to work in a much less structured environment, we need to show that we can do what we're asking them to do, and are true to our word. How do we do this?

Set clear boundaries

When we lead with empathy we need to be flexible and put firm boundaries in place so work does not drift. Our teams need to understand what's expected and when to deliver. It's not necessarily fair or kind to just allow people to do what they like as long as they get the job done; some team members will need your guidance and a framework to perform well. They need to know what is acceptable and what is not.

Inevitably there will be a need to find some common times when everyone is available for client-facing projects or team meetings; discuss this with your team and find a way forward.

Here's a series of key lessons we've learnt at MCM that can really help your team establish that division that they perhaps took for granted in an office:

Create a productive work space

The temporary work environments many of us created and adapted to during lockdown are not acceptable if we are to spend more time working from home long term. We may have members of staff who are living in shared accommodation or working from their bedroom.

We need our team members to have an environment that enables them to be productive.

Regardless of how happy they say they are with their environment it's essential you check how often they leave the room!

Consider their wellbeing. I've heard plenty of stories where young people in particular are moving from bed to desk to PlayStation and only leaving the room to eat or drink. Our role as empathetic leaders has to be to check in with each team member regularly; make sure they are supporting their own mental health by getting outside, taking breaks and separating their work and personal life (things we took for granted before now need to be part of our role).

Flexible office working

Encourage people to work from different locations regularly. We pay for our team to use flexible office space if they don't want to travel to one of our hubs but do want to get out of the house for a day. In fact, we hugely encourage them not to work alone for a solid five days in any week whenever possible. Not only does this mean a healthier, happier team but also has the benefit of opening up networking and learning opportunities that we lose from not being in an office environment. Even just seeing what people from other companies are doing in these shared spaces, having a chat at the coffee area and being around other people can give that boost and connection we once felt we needed every day.

Make your office disappear

Leaders who have worked remotely for years told me it's essential to make your office space disappear at the end of the working day and at weekends. Not everyone has the benefit of a home office where they can close the door and walk away. Those working from dining room tables or kitchens enjoyed their location, but at the end of the day their routine was to tidy work-related items into a cupboard or cover them up; this gives a clear signal to the brain that the work day is complete, and serves as a blocker to the unconscious drift back for a quick check of email.

Enjoy regular breaks

Regular breaks of five minutes every hour make a huge difference to wellbeing and productivity. One well-known method is the Pomodoro technique, which was invented by Italian Francesco Cirillo who said: "*I discovered that you could learn how to improve your effectiveness and be better able to estimate how long a task will take to complete by recording how you utilise your time.*"[20]

The process involves tackling tasks in short bursts of activity, typically 25 to 30 minutes then taking a two to five minute break. After four sessions you take a longer break of up to an hour then repeat the process until the end of your working day. This doesn't work for every task. Most of us have tasks we like to get stuck into and once in the zone can keep going for a couple of hours, but it is the theory of the technique that is important. We need to teach our teams to focus on one task, turning off all distractions then rewarding themselves with a break. Planning and breaking down days as much as possible has a huge effect

---

[20] *Francesco Cirillo, (2018), The Pomodoro Technique: The Acclaimed Time-Management System That Has Transformed How We Work, Currency, illustrated edition*

on productivity. Encourage them to make time to go for a walk: it really does make a world of difference.

Dodge the rabbit hole

In 1998, the year after I started MCM, email was still such a novelty that a romantic comedy titled *You've Got Mail* was released starring Tom Hanks and Meg Ryan. Today it could well be the subject of a horror story!

It's becoming more and more normal to respond to email at all hours of the day, but it's not doing anyone any favours.

Where I used to be able to catch up on admin on a Sunday morning (safe in the knowledge I'd have no interruptions) I now increasingly find I reply to an email and find that person responds straight back (which then drags you into a conversation that means your admin time disappears as if it was a regular working day).

The answer is simple: turn email off! But, going cold turkey is stressful and agitates our chimp.

We need to create a gradual shift where we encourage our team to turn it off in between regular checks. You can use the following checklist as a starting point if this is a challenge you are only just getting to grips with. Weaning yourself and your team off having email constantly open and feeling you need to always reply and always have an empty inbox will totally transform productivity.

Digital health check

Checking email once an hour so your team can ensure that what's in their inbox is not urgent.

- Close email down in between scheduled checks
  – this is crucial.

- Let your clients know if they have an urgent query it is better for them to phone.

- Treat email like mail. Check in and send out messages a few times a day. People will thank you for not flooding their inbox, you will feel less stressed and your productivity levels will soar.

- When sending email make it clear you don't expect an immediate response if you are emailing at an unsociable time that happens to work for you.

- Tell your team what times of day or how often you check your email. Suggest they do the same.

- If you or your team really feel it's impossible to be out of contact then make something like WhatsApp your "contact me if urgent" tool. Then if something really does need an answer they can message you or you can message them. Using something like this instead of email really focuses people's minds on whether something really does need an urgent answer or not.

- Handled properly, I guarantee you productivity and team happiness will soar!

One version of an email footer that has been circulating for a few years and is currently used by some of the team at Amazon Web Services says:

"TRULY HUMAN NOTICE: Getting this email out of normal working hours? We work at a digitally-enabled relentless pace, which can disrupt our ability to sleep enough, eat right, exercise, and spend time with the people that matter most. I am sending you this email at a time that works for me. I only expect you to respond to it when convenient to you."

Will Morish, of events organisers Prism, told me he missed the natural cut-off of being able to finish his work on the train then step through his front door and leave email behind him during lockdown. He shared this simple and highly effective tip: *"I work upstairs so when I come down for lunch or at the end of the day I make myself leave my phone upstairs. That means my wife and son get my undivided attention without me constantly checking my screen."*

Protected time

Simon Timmis, of the Institution of Engineering, which employs more than 500 staff, told me: *"Every day from 12.30pm to 1.30pm we have a ban on internal meetings. It's rigorously enforced from the CEO all the way through the organisation. If you really have to do an external meeting you can, but we try to avoid it unless it is absolutely essential. People respect it because everybody does it. You are guaranteed an hour, where you are positively encouraged to go and do something for your wellbeing. It's making a huge difference to our teams."*

HSBC went one step further and announced "Zoom-free Fridays". Love them or loathe them, Zoom, Teams and Google Hangouts were a lifesaver for many of us in 2020. The problem is it became easy to fill every hour of the day with a meeting where in a face-to-face world we would have had many natural breaks in between.

I wrote a tongue in cheek article at the start of the lockdown about Zoom neck and Zoom fatigue. But both soon became a common and almost accepted part of life.

They can definitely be more exhausting than we imagined:

- The millisecond lag time means it takes more concentration and effort to hold a meeting over video.

- Instead of making small talk and building rapport by shaking hands or having a coffee together we jump straight onto another online meeting without time to process or follow up any actionables. It can feel disrespectful and adds a time pressure that didn't exist before when we might block out an entire morning to go and see a client and be present with them.

As a leader you have the opportunity to create and reinforce new habits that support creativity, productivity and balance.

Phased return

In-person meetings have thankfully returned but remote meetings are here to stay. Just as we encourage flexible working, encourage a hybrid of in-person and remote meetings and routinely discuss how your team members feel with it all. Our first post-lockdown face-to-face meetings in London were exhilarating but also a shock to the system. Everyone felt shattered the next day through a combination of being up early, getting ready, commuting, chatting and of course the excitement of getting out! Things we once did every day will take time to re-establish as habits and, when hybrid, an entirely new habit may need to be developed.

Also, consider adding phone calls into the blend for internal and external communication. A phone conversation can fill some people with an instant sense of relief; it's less intrusive and can even feel more personal.

Building Your Culture

One of the concerns often cited around hybrid or WFA policies is that the company's culture will suffer. However, this begs the question, "What is your culture?" Does your company currently have a culture that your team identifies with and that is communicated to your customers?

As our work environments change, we need to adapt in more ways than just where we are physically working and how we are communicating. However, if you have a strong company culture, this should transcend the details around where and how you physically work. A strong company culture comes through in the way your team interacts with one another and your clients. It is about far more than whether you have a games room or funky graphics on the walls.

That said, it's still important to be mindful of how changes to the working environment could have an impact on those in your team. What did they sign up for and how do they feel about this new world we've all found ourselves in?

Part 3

In this part of the book I invite you to think about your working environment and to examine and define your culture. I'm also going to share how you can strengthen your company culture so that you have an enthused and productive team and happy customers.

The Where and When to Work Debate

Over the next decade the impact of the pandemic will continue to have huge effects on all areas of our lives. We will hopefully have learnt many lessons and not be tempted to simply default back to all of our old ways. Whilst we missed the ability to travel whenever we liked and meet people without having to think about it, many people also realised many of their journeys had been unnecessary. Car, train and plane journeys for short meetings or to attend events that could be just as easily carried out on screen meant pollution levels fell and productivity increased. Many people I spoke to said they are looking forward to being far more selective about the meetings they travel to and expect to go forward with a much better balance of what is necessary in person (both for work and happiness) and what can be done remotely in a fraction of the time, leaving more time for other enriching activities.

Chapter 9

The debate between those who insist back to office is best, those who want to try hybrid and those who want WFA is causing a shift in the employment market that we have maybe never seen the likes of. People have tasted that forbidden fruit of working from home totally guilt free. In many businesses, for many years, working from home had an associated stigma that meant you weren't going to be working at full pace. Many leaders had trust issues that teams couldn't be as productive or enthused from home but were quickly proved wrong.

For team members, the fact that everyone was remote meant there was no guilt or feeling they were an outsider. You all had the same amount of work to get through and, if you already had a dedicated and enthused team, everyone wanted to play their part and do their very best. Productivity increased in many areas as routines were established and many realised they were not only more effective but also had that extra time at the start and end of the day when they were no longer travelling.

Many companies are now insisting they will return to the office either full time or three to four days a week. This is more often driven by management rather than team choice, leaders who are certain their business can only truly thrive with everyone in an office. This may be driven by results or productivity studies of their performance over the previous 12 months or it may simply be a gut reaction to what they feel is right, or worse, what they want to be right.

In a world that is going to give employees much more choice of how, where and when they can work, it is this stance that is going to see many simply voting with their feet and moving to the type of culture they prefer.

We can truly lead with empathy by creating clear working policies that support our current staff and enable potential new recruits to effectively gauge if we are the right employer and team for them.

The pandemic has been the catalyst that demanded a change in working culture. When you as a leader redefine how the future of your team will look, it's inevitable that you will have staff who want to leave and new people who want the work-life scenario that you are offering.

Here's what we know so far:

- Remote meetings are here to stay.

- Many organisations saw an increase in productivity due to home working.

- There are people who want to return to full-time office working.

- There are people who love working from anywhere and want to continue.

- There are people who want a hybrid working arrangement.

- Our teams want the flexibility to choose.

- Some team members need to or want to be micromanaged; others flourished with free rein.

- Some people have luxury home offices; others are in shared accommodation.

- Some people used their new-found freedom from commuting to learn new skills, spend more time with family; other people experienced poor mental health, became overworked and felt isolated.

A truly empathetic leader will be in tune with their team whether they're in front of you or far away. Leading with empathy will bring much-needed reassurance and security to any team.

It's time to re-evaluate what has worked well over the past year and discuss and adopt new practices. When you're clear on what you're offering your team, your team will be clear on whether it's right for them or not. This process will create a strong, bonded, productive team that shares values and purpose.

Time to Redefine the Working Environment

There is no definitive answer to what is the right way to to work; it will differ for each organisation and between teams. However, what is clear from the pandemic is that people have tasted the freedom of working from anywhere. For some it was poison; for others, a delight.

As leaders we are faced with very different potential working environments that will affect the working culture either positively or negatively. Either way, it requires careful consideration.

In addition to your shared values and beliefs, the way in which your teams work (remote, in office, hybrid, WFA) will heavily influence who joins your team and who remains with your organisation. If someone has found a quality of life they love by working mainly from home, it's going to be very hard for them to give that up to return to a daily office life, no matter how solid your shared beliefs are (or even how much you pay).

Likewise, someone who has missed the daily commute, the joy of daily social interaction and the structure of a 9 to 5 office routine will be desperate to return to a role that provides this.

Evolution of new working practices

Making this distinction is paramount to evolving as a team but also fraught with risks. If you or your organisation decide remote is the way forward and your team gradually adapts around this model, what then happens if you need to reverse this decision and return to office life? You may lose good employees, and will almost certainly have recruited from locations too far for a regular commute.

So, how do we choose the best option? The choice may not be fully in your control. If you're a business owner you have much more choice, but as a team leader in even the largest organisations you still need to make the case for what is the right decision for your team. A marketing team may have different needs and personalities to a sales team or a production team; if you don't try to establish the best environment for each team it will be hard to keep that joint motivation (at worst, you will struggle to retain key members or attract the best talent).

Team input

As empathetic leaders we will need to find out how our existing team members feel about a new working regime. What do they want to do? How do they feel about working remotely?

What would be their ideal balance? Why are they in favour of one over the over?

Throughout the pandemic we at MCM surveyed our team through a system called Office Vibe .

We regularly took the temperature, and still do today, of how people were feeling, what ideas and suggestions they had, what they didn't like and also regularly checked in to see how many days they wanted to work, and how they felt about their new working environment (largely, that was from home during the pandemic!).

A shifting culture

During the pandemic our team at MCM was collectively saving an average of 600 hours a month by not travelling to and from the office each day. They were spending more time on their hobbies and staying fit, and they consistently generated fantastic results for our clients.

Our monthly office surveys went from everyone hoping the future would maybe allow one day a week working from home to 90 per cent saying they felt one day a week maximum in a fixed office and regular team socials would be their utopia going forward.

MCM has always had a really close-knit and sociable team with regular lunch time games, lunches, walks and groups meeting up after work. My expectation had been that the younger members would crave a full return, and those with families, a partial return. The overwhelming response has been that as a team we still want to be able to interact throughout the day (chat through WhatsApp and Teams about our latest challenge or the films we've watched), meet up in person to innovate and socialise, have regular offsite fun 'bonding' events, but, perhaps surprisingly, we also want to work from home. It works for us and it works for our clients.

In a changing world we can expect to see employees voting with their feet and moving to a work culture that suits them personally.

What did employees sign up for?

The reality is that if you have employed people who want to come to a big glass building each day that has a slide in the middle of it or a games room full of energetic colleagues and you suddenly take that away and instruct them to work from their bedroom for the rest of their working life, you will lose staff. At the very least you will completely demoralise people. In days gone by leaders might have jumped into a new way of working and enforced it, but that's not leading with empathy.

The sticking point will be that not everyone in your team will want exactly the same thing. You are unlikely to reach consensus. Some people might not have the discipline to work from home long term. Looking at another company and deciding to emulate what they do will set you up for failure; their team is not your team.

Their leader is not you. You must build a new working model with your team and continue to review it.

Working from home was once eyed with suspicion. Without supervision and watchful eyes it was thought that people would sit in their pyjamas, take longer lunch breaks and clock off early. Home working was considered 'skiving' and a last resort that was allowed with great reluctance and only on rare occasions due to the fear that productivity would drop.

However, it's become far more clear that when your team is happy and knows that they have some control over the working process, they will be working in the right place for them which means, and we've seen this through MCM, they perform at their best and deliver better customer service because they are happy in the workplace, and you will continue to deliver fantastic results.

When your team feels fully trusted and listened to, which really doesn't depend on whether you're office based, remote or WFA, they will always perform to their full potential.

The MCM working structure

Our WFA culture works around hubs, flexible workspaces, weekly face-to-face meetups for those close enough to a hub, regular team socials and a quarterly full team face to face. We encourage our team members to work away from their homes several times a week as a minimum if possible. When they are working in a hub we try to ensure several members of the team join them.

We also encourage them to go together and experience remote workspaces where they'll be surrounded by others. Some of these people will be in a similar industry to ours; others, completely different as we rotate locations. This gives them experience with other types of people, helps them gain knowledge from those around them, helps generate great ideas they hear from other remote workers that they can then bring back to us and of course gives them the social life they may miss out on by not being 9 to 5.

For days when people are at home we use a tool called Coffee Roulette (see resources page for details) where people are randomly assigned to a colleague for a virtual coffee break. No work talk is allowed. This encourages spontaneous chat and reduces any feelings of isolation.

Our way of working takes more planning and encouragement from us than just the old style contract where you came to the office daily as the norm, but, in my opinion, the opportunities that this style of work presents and the potential quality of life far outweigh the negatives. I'll be sharing more about MCM's work culture in the next chapter.

To help you decide your ideal format, the pros and cons for each of the working models that came through from my interviews included:

Pros of office based – '9 to 5'

- Quick and efficient communication happens naturally without scheduling
- Instantly get a feel for issues arising (cliques forming or a drop in morale)
- Long life is associated with strong social ties we get from being together
- Strong bonds form, making loyalty and long service more likely
- Creativity, ideas and challenges are sometimes easier in an in-person group
- Ideas flow between teams through chance encounters
- It's familiar
- Staff are provided with equipment they need so feel looked after
- Will attract new talented people who want this structure
- Ability to manage teams and workflow
- Fully engaged and lively workforce
- Transfer of skills, learning and knowledge from experienced team members
- Enhanced social skills
- Emotional support
- Social life.

Cons of being office based '9 to 5'

- Multiple distractions and constant interruptions
- Travel time to and from work
- Productivity can tank quite quickly
- For some people childcare issues arise
- Now it's up to the leaders to make a compelling case as to why people must be physically present
- Rental or running costs for the organisation
- Potentially limits recruitment pool
- Can be more challenging for people with disabilities or health problems who prefer to be at home.

Pros of hybrid working

- Increased productivity
- Team members have an element of choice
- No-one has to travel every day
- Opportunity to attract new talent
- Likely to retain most of current workforce if they can choose what personally fits best
- Provides change of scene on demand, boosting creativity
- Expands recruitment pool
- Happier team = happier customers = better business.

Cons of hybrid working

- Cliques might form if certain groups of people are in on different days
- Less atmosphere as there will inevitably be empty desks
- Takes more organisation and management
- Feeling among those who are at home that they are less likely to be valued or receive positive appraisals
- Fear of missing out for those who aren't in the office.

The hybrid model is potentially one that can derail teams quicker than any other. It is trying to get the best of both worlds, allowing freedom and flexibility but to work it requires a high level of structure and timetabling. This can then quickly go against the purpose of being hybrid and cause more conflict and uncertainty than it takes away. It is the model that many companies believe they will adopt without fully thinking through the implications. It feels like it is a solution that will suit everyone, but is definitely the model to be approached with the most caution and consideration.

Pros of working from anywhere

- Businesses can utilise hubs at multiple locations for meetings and collaboration that's best in person
- Increased loyalty and staff retention
- Employees save on commuting costs
- Team members can live where they want
- Creates flexibility for families with children, enabling more quality time
- Will attract new talent
- Work-life balance has potential to improve
- In-person meetings and gatherings are valued
- Inclusivity – diverse workforce based anywhere in the world bringing fresh perspectives that you may otherwise not have been privy to.

Cons of working from anywhere

- Harder to manage
- How will this impact on graduates and new employees who need early support?
- Perceived threat to team culture (evidence from past year shows minimal threat and in the next chapter I share a story that shows how our culture at MCM has actually become stronger)
- Will not work for every type of team or organisation
- Less socialising within the team
- Feel isolated or left out.

Chapter 10

Many large organisations, including companies like Spotify, have recently announced that all their staff can choose where they want to work, saying they believe:

- Work isn't something you come to the office for; it's something you do.
- Effectiveness can't be measured by the number of hours people spend in an office (instead, giving people the freedom to choose where they work will boost effectiveness).
- Giving our people more flexibility will support better work-life balance and help tap into new talent pools whilst keeping our existing band members.
- Operating as a distributed organisation will produce better and more efficient ways of working through more intentional use of communication and collaboration practices, processes and tools.

The problem child

The major consideration that will continue to be the subject of much debate is career development for school leavers, graduates and an inexperienced workforce in general. Whilst working remotely may well suit many of us that have families and plenty of space in which to set up a home office, it definitely doesn't suit the vast majority of young people starting out in their careers. Working from a bedroom at home or a shared flat is no fun and certainly not good for mental health long term.

Working in an office away from home is so much more than simply learning how to do your job. It is learning life skills from those around you, picking up knowledge from the experience of people who have been working longer than you and enjoying a social life with those who work around you during the day, at lunchtime and after work. Many of us met our partners through work-related socialising and formed lifelong friendships in our early working lives through shared events and memories.

As empathetic leaders we have a moral obligation to think about the needs of the people we want to work for us. How would you feel if you were fresh out of school or university and suddenly, instead of being surrounded by lively peers, you were working from perhaps your parents home or shared accommodation? When people interact with people in person there's an opportunity for spontaneous inspiration and to grow and express themselves not just professionally but personally.

As we grow and learn we develop a sense of purpose of what's right and wrong, but much of this is learnt through interacting with work colleagues. No matter how committed a 20 year old might appear, when they work from home there will never be the same routine of getting up early, getting dressed smartly, sitting in traffic for an hour or on a sweaty train and turning up on time no matter what they did the night before.

Yes, there is the attraction that WFA means you can truly become a digital nomad (and this may appeal to some for a while) but the practicalities of this working for many are slim. For the vast majority of school leavers and graduates the preference will be to work with others daily (or more often than not) and that presents a challenge to any non 9 to 5 working models.

Again, for your culture to succeed and grow, empathetic leaders will need to be clear from the outset which of the categories your team will be expected to adhere to because this will give them the security, boundaries and understanding of what is expected from them, all of which makes your role as leader more fulfilling. If you want to attract school leavers and graduates then you will more than likely need office space for them. Some companies will get by using colocation spaces, but whatever the venue they will need experienced members of their team also going to this space regularly or none of the transferred learning will occur.

In addition, the location factor gives several other important areas to consider.

Remote onboarding

Remote onboarding (the process of incorporating a new employee into a company and familiarising them with the company culture and policies) has become a fairly simple exercise when employing team members who have already worked in an office and are on the next stage of their career. Many job skills and tasks can be taught remotely as well, but new, young team members who are starting out in employment may need exposure to a range of levels of experience and years worked to also learn the life skills that naturally develop in a face-to-face environment.

To do this you need face-to-face time and that means that, at the very minimum, you will need multiple more senior team members who will be happy to regularly work in the office space to act as teachers and mentors.

A level of supervision will also be needed or, as one interviewee pointed out to me, it could just become an office full of new starters and you could end up with the equivalent of a "giant creche" or something resembling a university halls of residence free-for-all that will not work for either learning or productivity. Remember, some people need and want some form of supervision and guidance, and no more so than people fresh to working life.

Remote hiring during and post pandemic

During the challenges of Covid-19, we hired five members of staff. The interviews were remote so we had not met the people in person. As soon as possible after they joined, we invited them to the office for a meeting with a small group of us so that they felt fully integrated.

Our furthest UK team member lives in Cornwall and MCM was originally based in Kent, so a daily commute would never be feasible. Instead, we agreed that, as a minimum, they will be at all our quarterly meetups and, from time to time, any events in between that really need face to face. MCM pays for their train fare and accommodation because it's really important to us that they are fully integrated, and that we deepen our working relationships. It's often very different when you meet someone in the flesh too; you don't tend to ask someone's height in an interview so boy, were we surprised!

Attracting new talent

You may decide you are happy only employing people with experience who have already 'served' their office time and are now ready for hybrid or WFA. Indeed there are companies already capitalising on the remote trend by doing the opposite and snapping up what has now become more affordable office space and kitting them out with Google-like facilities that will attract school leavers and graduates. They are the companies that need young, energetic and fresh talent for emerging technologies or social media campaigns and PR aimed at youth audiences. They are happy to attract and train the talent, maybe in the clear knowledge that there then comes a point where many of their staff want to move on to a WFA company. Maybe that is also part of the plan to only retain a core team that is fresh and engaged

Others, like Tamara Littleton from The Social Element, say that the young staff they attract come because of the flexibility this type of working gives them. She said: "*More and more young people are seeing working from home as a bonus. Some of the people that we have, who are in their 20s, like doing several things. So they've got the job with The Social Element, but they're also doing their own side hustle. And, you know, I think there has been a bit of a push for people who like that flexibility. We have a lot of creative people in the agency because we're creating content on behalf of brands.*

"They are the ones doing TikTok etc and they're out and about, they're creating content, but they're also maybe just creating videos and images or whatever. Those people often don't want to even be full-time employed by us. They like the fact that they can work across multiple agencies, and they've chosen that lifestyle of being a freelance creative. The world has changed and this is an active choice for many, many people, including young people."

Diversity and opportunities

Not surprisingly, many of the WFA or remote companies I spoke to said they had more job applications from people with disabilities than traditional office based businesses, because they knew they could work from home and avoid a regular or challenging commute. They also hired more parents, single parents and carers who may previously have had to choose between work and being a stay-at-home parent.

There is also more inclusivity because organisations are able to employ people around the world (or even just from other ends of the country) who can offer brand new cultural perspectives and ways of working. People living in less affluent areas, or who choose to relocate due to their partner's job for example, face fewer limitations in how they work.

Tamara of The Social Element told me she calls it "accidental diversity", in that the WFA model has meant that they can attract talent from anywhere, from any background, from any culture, of any age and of any physical ability, resulting in a business with a diverse and dynamic skillbase.

Previously, with the WFA model being more unusual, the job pool was limited for many of these hugely talented people. Now with WFA or at least flexible working becoming the norm, not only will that range of jobs hugely expand for them but also open our businesses up to talent we may never before have been able to access.

Leading with empathy also includes putting yourselves in the shoes of your current and future team members. You need to understand your current team's preference. Does this fit with yours or your business as a whole? But also, and equally as importantly, you need to consider a broader awareness of where new team members will come from in future and who you really want to attract.

Chapter 10

How Do We Define Our Work Culture?

A well-defined culture that all members of the team understand, subscribe to and embody is an essential component of a successful business. If it was important in the 9 to 5 world then it is paramount in a world where you can work from anywhere. Effective teamwork starts with a great organisational culture, no matter where or how you operate. But what do we mean by work culture?

At its most basic, a work culture is defined by how a company interacts with its employees, how the employees interact with each other and how both in turn interact with their customers.

There was a time not so long ago when culture seemed to be defined by how many pool tables and Nespresso machines your office had. Talk of Google having slides in their office, ball pits and bean bags was peppered throughout the press (and heralded as the future of office culture). A 2008 article on BBC News[21] has the headline *Google your way to a wacky office*, and

---

[21] Jane Wakefield, (2008), "Google your way to a wacky office", BBC News, 13 March,

a few years later, with many companies jumping on the band-wagon of the culture of the future, *Business Insider*[22] even had an article titled *RANKED: The Best Slides And Worst Slides In Google's Offices*.

Follow the trend

As a marketing agency we followed the trends and duly installed table tennis, a PlayStation, pool, air hockey and a variety of games. We even installed artificial grass across an entire floor of our building where the games room was built, having seen Innocent Smoothies do the same.

All these remained throughout our 9 to 5 existence and they were used by some more than others. They were appreci-ated, they looked good on social media and gave an area where people generally went to have lunch together, with the games being peripheral. In fact, like kids at Christmas who prefer the cardboard box to the toy inside, we soon found the most popular game was 'ball in the bin'. This involved the large games room bin, with swing lid removed and a PVC football. The team – nearly everyone wanted to be part of every game – would stand in a circle around the bin and play keepy uppy around random people in the circle, then after a certain number of touches the ball had to be aimed at the bin and a score would be a direct hit.

---

[22] *Matt Lynley, (2012), "RANKED: The Best Slides And Worst Slides In Google's Offices", Business Insider, 14 May,*

Bringing people together

If a games room could ever help our culture or I needed any further confirmation we had a greatly bonded team, this did it for me. Over and above the existence of the games room, table tennis or astroturf, the ball in the bin game truly became something that brought the team together, totally away from their work, had a combined and central aim and was something they all got a thrill from doing. It also saw stronger skilled footballers help the more useless ones (like me) with easy passes (and a combined roar of satisfaction when the ball hit the bin).

With much regret, after many years the game had to be moved to the car park on health and safety grounds after the ball hitting the ceiling dislodged the fluorescent lighting grids one too many times, but 'ball in the bin' is still a phrase that will bring a light of excitement and wistful look to the faces of team members past and present.

Shared purpose

It wasn't the games room or the game that **created** that culture though. That was a small part of our culture. The game, on a very basic level, gave the team a common purpose that brought them together, excited them and gave them a sense of achievement when accomplished. They played that game together because they shared a common bond and goal (no pun intended!). They all loved their jobs and knew exactly what they were trying to achieve for our clients. They knew they were given the freedom to work their way, and had the support of the team if they couldn't solve an issue on their own.

Above all, they were, and of course still are, nice people who genuinely care about each other. In addition to other team members this naturally filters down to what our clients experience. Our feedback is always that the team is a great bunch of people to work with. They get great results (which should really be a given), but they also truly want to please and build friendships with their customers and understand what success really means for them. They keep things simple and don't try to confuse through jargon or technical terms. If you want to hear popular phrases such as "Blue Sky Thinking", we've never been that agency, and never will be.

We've always been at pains to explain acronyms and phrases such as ROI, CRO, BMM, Ad Extensions and Phrase match. Part of our purpose is to share our knowledge and help people understand what we do. We even teach our clients how to do our job if they want to know. Our belief in transparency and openness builds longer lasting and more enjoyable client relationships. Right from the start, part of our culture has included that we're human beings supporting human beings; jargon has no place in our communication.

A personal fail

I have to admit we did sort of fail on one particular occasion though. We were giving a talk called DIY SEO (do it yourself search engine optimisation). We had advertised the talk and had a full house in a recently restored old fire station. There was a mixed audience of both corporates and small businesses. Halfway through it was time for a break, but before we paused I asked if anyone in the audience had any burning questions. A hand went up and a man who turned out to be a retired business consultant asked, "Yes, could you tell me what SEO stands for?"

The whole talk had been about search engine optimisation up to that point. Every slide carried that phrase and we had naturally assumed anyone attending such a talk would be well aware of what the letters SEO stood for. It was an awkward moment met with the nervous pockets of muted laughter you get in a packed room. I'm still not sure which of us that was directed at more but we had certainly missed our own 'jargon fully explained' test. **Lesson learnt!**

Culture survives outside 9 to 5

Just because we don't go into the office every day doesn't mean our culture has suffered. Many people are mistakenly worried that no 9 to 5 means no culture. That simply isn't the case; it just takes a bit more planning.

Every morning our various teams meet via Zoom and highlight what they're working on that day. We have a full team Zoom meeting on a Tuesday morning, and on Friday afternoons we finish at 4pm with a team Zoom where we talk rubbish and play even worse games. It's a wind down and something nobody wants to drop, even post lockdowns. Once a month on a Friday, as many of the team as are able work from one of the hubs and then go for face-to-face beers afterwards.

We find huge value and enjoyment still in face-to-face get togethers and our Culture Club (I didn't name it!) finds suitable venues for us to meet. They might encourage groups of people or, occasionally, everyone to come into the office on a particular day because experience showed us that otherwise people drift in or out and we don't know when to expect them.

Booking system

Now we also have a booking system for the office so everyone can see who is going to be there and when. We might see a maximum of six people working together in the office in the morning, going out for lunch and then working from home in the afternoon. When people feel excluded they begin to lose interest so we have payday beers which are face to face as often as possible, and if people cannot attend our quarterly meetup they will receive a voucher, or if we're out for pizza we'll have a pizza delivered to their house.

Shared office

Twice a month at least, and again it's optional, we will go to shared office space in Shoreditch, or London Bridge, so the team can experience something different. I encourage this as much as possible because creativity increases when we experience different environments and there are more opportunities to network with people. For some of our team it's a chance to dress up a bit and can even feel like a day out. It works extremely well for them. More often than not they'll stop and have a beer on the way home. They're always full of smiles the next day and that's enough face-to-face interaction for them to feed off for the next couple of weeks.

I see the benefits that this type of culture creates and empathetic leaders will do well to encourage this. All too often we might not feel like going out for dinner with friends, but when you go you feel so much better for it; these team get togethers are the same.

As leaders we need to recognise that people need encouragement; in many ways they need a facilitator so they have access to these opportunities without them being compulsory.

Keep your finger on the pulse

MCM has always had a good working culture and it's now the strongest it's ever been, but, as with any business, you need to keep your finger on the pulse and adapt to changing circumstances.

We used to do a morning stand up where someone would write on a whiteboard all the projects that were being done that day. We'd welcome input and comments but it was also about bringing people together.

We've adapted that now to use Click Up, which is a giant to-do list and calendar system that an entire team can use to manage tasks and time. We use this for our remote morning meetings and it's taught us how to use new tools which, over time, have also made us better at what we do.

The majority of people at MCM really like this way of working and living.

Productivity

As far as results go, at the time of writing we just set a record for our best-ever month in the past 25 years. We're finding different tools and different ways of doing things and this in turn is helping us be more productive.

Culture needn't be lost just because you're not in an office every day. It doesn't have to come from slogans on the walls. Human nature says you no longer notice those after a few days anyway.

It doesn't come from the decoration, the toys, the free food or the office dog; all these components are elements that complement your culture and help facilitate your team's interaction but they don't make the culture.

Many companies may think they have a culture that has evolved over the years as they naturally attract certain types of people and carry out certain types of work. If you ask their teams what that culture is, they may at best find it hard to define and at worst have a completely different interpretation of what it is. This can gradually create not only confused teams pulling in different directions but also a lack of true purpose and direction.

As I explained at the beginning of this chapter, at its very basic core, culture is defined by how a company interacts with its employees, how the employees interact with each other and how both in turn interact with their customers. No type of culture is necessarily the right culture. Different types work for different industries and, of course, different types of people.

Well-known work cultures

In a Harvard Business Review guide to corporate culture they gave the examples of online retailer Zappos as exemplifying a culture of enjoyment, the supermarket chain Whole Foods as a culture of purpose and Disney as one of caring. Lloyd's of London was defined as a culture of safety and pharma giant GSK (GlaxoSmithKline plc) as one of results. Each of these fits with what we, the consumers, would expect of those companies but also will attract certain types of people who want to work there.

Culture, it says, is the social order of an organisation, shaping attitudes and behaviour; put simply, it is what is encouraged, discouraged, accepted or rejected within a group. It can cover a combination of several elements including:

- Purpose
- Learning
- Caring
- Enjoyment
- Order
- Safety
- Results
- Authority

Before moving away from a 9 to 5 model, businesses need to decide whether their current culture fully supports any of the other working structures. If your culture is heavily dependent on authority and micromanagement, for instance, will it still work in a WFA environment?

Assuming your culture will adapt long term to a hybrid model (without some redefinition of what your culture really is) is a potential problem. During the pandemic government rulings meant that people had to work from home and had no choice but to accept the change. It didn't have to be part of the culture they were used to or were attracted to because it was a short-term (or so we thought) measure that we were told would save lives.

Chapter 11

Re-examining and, if necessary, redefining your culture for the post-pandemic world should focus on:

- **Working practices**

9 to 5, hybrid, WFA, fully remote. People now know they have choices and will choose what suits them best. They might prioritise how they can work over the purpose and values of your organisation. Your working practice will completely change the employee pool available to you and the type of people you attract.

- **Leadership style**

Leading in anything other than the traditional 9 to 5 takes an evolution in leadership style. Understanding, empathy and total trust to let people self manage for much of the time are core to the success of WFA and hybrid models. If your organisation and culture is built on a hierarchical and autocratic style of leadership, this may well not work outside of 9 to 5, or will at the least involve far more micromanagement than ever before.

- **Purpose, vision and values
  (more on this in the next chapter)**

Why does your organisation exist? What is the purpose of your team? What matters to you as a team? A clearly defined purpose motivates people to carry out the right actions, inspires and ultimately sets the values and behaviours that translate into the culture.

- **Communication**

How do you communicate core company values so the entire team continues sharing them and feeling part of them? How often you communicate as a team and, most importantly, how transparent you are in sharing information and making decisions is also key.

- **People**

What types of people are best suited and likely to be aligned to these values? What type of person will complement your team?

The cornerstone of any work culture is built on company values and purpose. But what are your company and team values, how do they impact your team and clients and why does your organisation even exist?

Let's explore some easy ways to redefine them in the next chapter.

Values and Purpose

As businesses and teams transition to new working hours and environments, redefining your culture is key to building and retaining an excellent and engaged team. With less emphasis on the daily office, the desk next to you and the group you wander off to lunch with, the true meaning of culture is exposed. We know it never should have been dressed up as slogans on walls, ping pong tables or a branded mug, but it now needs careful thought (and, crucially, buy-in from all of your team) if it is to survive and grow outside of the traditional 9 to 5.

The pandemic has jolted us awake and deepened our level of appreciation and desire to live life, no matter how we define that. We've learnt to appreciate even the smallest things that had just become the norm and were often unnoticed.

The MCM team was in Borough Market in London for our first post-lockdown quarterly meetup and one of them mentioned how she'd never take the experience of being able to wander and experience things like this for granted again. People are becoming much more conscious that even nibbling a tiny sample of chocolate brownie is important.

Life isn't all about work, work, work, but when we are working it's important that that work is engaging and fulfilling for us and all around us.

Covid-19 has accelerated this desire for balance and appreciation; the genie is out of the bottle. People want more purpose in their lives and real fulfilment that doesn't just come from sitting on a beach. Fulfilment is being valued and contributing to something bigger than you alone. It's all about your values and purpose.

If our work ethos was simply: *'We're a nice bunch of people that get great results and get on really well with our clients,'* then not only are we a definition of what every business should be, but we also give our team nothing to identify themselves with as to why they work at MCM rather than anywhere else. It's not compelling enough.

A **fantastic** culture is a product of the **shared** values, purpose, beliefs, attitudes and, ultimately, behaviours of a team. It results in how people work together towards a common goal, how they treat each other and, ultimately, how they treat their customers.

No matter what you believe your current culture is, or how well you believe it is embedded, this is a great time to at least check that it is still understood and embraced by all through shared values and purpose.

Chapter 12

Find your why

In author Simon Sinek's book, *Find Your Why*[23], he recommends you find your current values and purpose by getting clear on 'why' you do what you do.

This applies to us as individuals and to our teams and our organisations.

To find your **why** you must first look at **what** you do as an organisation and then **how** you do it (then finding the why should be why you and your team get up and work each day). Every single one of us is entitled to feel fulfilled by the work we do, to wake up feeling inspired to work, to feel safe when we're working and to end the day with a sense that we contributed to something larger than ourselves.

- Your **WHY** is your purpose, what you believe in and what you want to achieve as a team. It's the driving factor behind everything you do.

- Your **HOW** is what you do when you're at your best to bring the WHY to life.

- Your **WHAT** is the work you do and output of what you do and, ultimately, the products and service you deliver.

---

[23] *Simon Sinek, (2017), Find Your Why, Portfolio Penguin*

Chapter 12

Why your why matters more than ever

Employees working remotely even for only a fraction of the week need to know their own and the organisation's **why** more than ever. People need and want a sense of purpose, engagement and fulfilment. They want to be trusted, but also need daily guidance and inspiration. They want feedback and a chance to celebrate and be celebrated.

Fulfilment comes from a role that goes over and above simply earning a living. Engaged team members become so much more passionate about their jobs that the mundane tasks every role inevitably includes become easy to tackle. Disengagement and lack of purpose sets even the most brilliant staff up to fail.

Louise Dell, of European villa and an international property portal Kyero.com, told me that carrying out a **find your why** exercise with external consultant Sharon Collier from The Leadership School was transformational to her and her team. *"As a group we came away with the motto: 'We help people find their sunshine,' which we love. It feels perfect for what we want to do and fully relates to people buying a property abroad. But actually, it's so much more than that. As a team we want to help each other find our sunshine, as well as the customers we support.*

"This in turn becomes part of our culture and means the team naturally asks themselves how they can help their customers, whether that's estate agents, or buyers, or all their team members. How can we each help the other find their sunshine?"

Chapter 12

Live your Why

Stuart Miles, who founded Pocket-lint[24] (one of the first and longest running gadget review sites) back in 2003, told me he makes sure all his team are regularly reminded of their why: *"We inform and entertain on the tech that matters."* He told me it succinctly described what they do, and helps his team write better articles for their website.

---

[24] *https://www.pocket-lint.com/*

Simon Sinek's find your why process is available on his website[25], but the core process consists of:

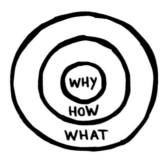

What

Establish what you do as a business and a team. List all your services or all of your products.

How

How do you deliver these? What sets you apart from anyone else that delivers them. How are you special?

Why

Why do you do what you do? What is the purpose, the cause or the belief for why your company and your team exists? This then forms the basis of your team's purpose and values.

This exercise might take weeks or months to really refine to the point that the whole team feels inspired and committed, but when you do the energy and excitement is palpable.

---

[25] *Simon Sinek, (2017), Find Your Why, Portfolio Penguin*

Team effort

A shared **why** that is jointly crafted through debate, discussion and reflection will:

- Inspire and motivate the team, giving them a clear understanding of their purpose
- Enable you to establish a core set of values that enable the why
- Give direction and focus
- Help the team go from good to great
- Become the core of your brand and communication
- Shape your customer service policy
- Give you clear values to recruit against
- Retain a productive, happy and highly engaged team
- Define your culture.

Your 'why' and your associated values should be the driver of how you treat, communicate, share, include and spread trust throughout your team. They go beyond simply a mission statement and will soon be seen through if they are simply a written list. Great culture comes from really living a shared 'why': the values and the purpose of a team.

Revisit your why

As a team we revisit our 'why', our values and our purpose regularly. At the heart of our 'why' has always been the central element that MCM has lived by for the past 24 years: *A happy team = happy customers*

Chapter 12

Our customers are hugely important to us, but we are nothing without an inspired and happy team. People who are proud to be doing what they are doing, and who understand why they are doing it, will naturally deliver better customer service and incredible results.

As we embraced the WFA concept fully we realised that the word HAPPY just wasn't enough. Happy means something different to everyone. So we needed to understand just what it was that made us all so inspired every day to be part of the MCM team. What could we say to potential new employees and new customers that made them realise just what working for us or with us means?

Refresh your why

Our latest 'why' session was led by our HR consultant. Although she knows the team well, she isn't part of the day-to-day business (it's helpful to have someone external to your team to lead this).

She asked that I say very little. I wasn't allowed into any of the break out groups. This had to be about 'the team'. This is a great piece of advice that really helped the process flow.

Simon Sinek in his original *Why TED Talk*[26] used the example of how Apple started with their 'why', enabling them to be one of the best-selling brands of all time. They outsold all other more established (and arguably more qualified) PC and tech companies.

---

[26] Simon Sinek, (2009), How great leaders inspire action, TEDxPuget Sound

Chapter 12

If Apple started with a 'what', Simon Sinek explained, they may have said something like: " 'We make great computers. They're user-friendly, beautifully designed, and easy to use. Want to buy one?' But instead, starting with their why, they said: 'With everything we do, we aim to challenge the status quo. We aim to think differently. Our products are user-friendly, beautifully designed, and easy to use. We just happen to make great computers. Want to buy one?' A far more compelling proposition for both customers and team members alike."

Theresa, our consultant, started our most recent session by encouraging the team to think beyond what they do day to day and look at the wider why of MCM. She shared the story of when President John F. Kennedy visited the NASA space centre in 1962. He noticed a janitor carrying a broom and said:

"Hi, I'm Jack Kennedy. What are you doing?"

"Well, Mr. President," the janitor responded, "I'm helping put a man on the moon."

It's a simple yet very powerful story that shows that no matter who you are in an organisation, you are part of the 'why' and the 'what.'

Remote success

Our session was facilitated over Zoom so all our team members could be involved in the process. Our people were far more open, honest and expressive behind the safety of their cameras than they might have been if in one room together.

Our HR consultant had warned us there would be fun, laughter and tears. I thought she was joking, but within the first hour we'd had tears from several team members who were genuinely over-whelmed with pride at some of the stories they shared. It even took them by surprise, but, such is the closeness of our team, it wasn't awkward (and none of those who had expressed their feelings felt the need to leave the room to compose themselves! They took a few deep breaths and continued).

Discovering your why

The session circled around three areas:

- Team members shared specific stories of when they felt most proud to work for MCM.
- In each of these stories, they then identified the specific contribution MCM made to the lives of others.
- Then they shared what the contribution of MCM allowed others to go and do or be.

The day included breakout rooms, feeding back what was discussed and then dividing into two teams (each taking every thought recorded from the day on virtual post-it notes!) and creating a WHY statement.

Even though the teams were kept separate, both produced almost identical statements.

As empathetic leaders it's good to see how a session like this not only brings a team closer together and inspires healthy debate but also helps people realise what they are truly passionate about. When they're given the opportunity to reflect, they realise how much their work and their role at MCM matter to them (hence the tears!).

The professional why is personal

The 'why' is not intended to be a mission statement on a wall, or an elevator pitch.

It needs to be explained, expanded and actioned; it's something the whole team has contributed to and believes in. It is unique.

Whilst it's nice for your clients to see what is at the core of your team, the true purpose is to strengthen your team's shared belief and purpose, which in turn helps attract the right talent and supports your team in making the right choice when recruiting (this is explored further in Chapter 13).

Refining your why

Our 'why' statement was jointly refined and expanded until we had something the whole team felt really invested in.

Our most up to date 'why' became:

"To challenge and inspire growth so we thrive and exceed expectations whilst empowering people to live their best lives."

By 'best lives' the team meant a work-life balance that left them inspired, fulfilled and constantly challenged professionally yet also allowed time for them to indulge in hobbies, family and 'me time' in equal quantities. It also meant supporting everyone around us to live whatever their 'best life' looked like, including contributing to the lives of our customers by bringing them amazing results and a hugely personal service.

Was it too cheesy?

We spent days agonising over 'best lives' and one team member raised her fingers in the air to signify quotation marks and in a squeaky voice said: *"hashtag best lives!"*

Were we being too cheesy? Did it sound authentic? But the more we delved into it, the more we realised that everyone in the team was fully invested in the statement.

Keep your why alive

Once you've established your 'why', your values and your purpose and everyone is fully embracing and living by them, they need to be kept alive. They will only benefit your team if they are regularly discussed and are actually lived by on a daily basis. In the WFA world it's even more crucial. Regularly communicating, sharing and celebrating when people truly live by them is essential.

Tamara Littleton formed the social media agency The Social Element[27] back in 2002. She has a team of more than 350 people across the world and has always been a WFA agency with hubs in cities such as London, Valencia and New York.

---

[27] *https://thesocialelement.agency/*

She believes it is their team culture that attracts and retains talent even though she has such a large and remote team.

She said: "*We focus a great deal on our values and we got people to help us come up with them. We talk about them a lot. They aren't just written down and forgotten; we employ people using our values, and we reward people using them too in the all hands when we do shoutouts. I think that's a key thing. There's a lot more celebration of people's successes, I think, in that particular sort of style. There's lots of congratulating people in front of the team when someone does a great job on a project, but also where that shows how they're living the values. We also have a very transparent approach. We share the numbers as well as how much money we're making. This is the profit. We're very open and transparent. And I think we've created a culture that the team can ask anything at all and we're totally open.*"

When a team has shared values and purpose it is unstoppable. Obstacles become unimportant, they know why they're doing what they do and they're driven to do it for the customers and for themselves.

The notion that stepping out of a 9 to 5 office and working from anywhere will destroy your team culture or impact on its values is clearly unfounded. If you're working in a way that makes you feel proud and happy then there is so much personal satisfaction and fulfilment nurturing you as a person and as a leader. When you're managing a team that is genuinely happy and you don't have to crack the whip all day, it enables you to be even more empathetic because you're less stressed.

MCM is thriving, and Tamara's business, The Social Element, has run a WFA policy for two decades and they're stronger than ever. With a shared vision, team members naturally support each other, and, as the TEAM saying goes, *together everyone achieves more*.

Hiring Aligned to Your Culture and Values

One of the key benefits of establishing your values and purpose and defining your work culture is that it enables you to recruit new people who live and breathe the same values as the rest of your team. You can easily communicate your work culture in job adverts and demonstrate it through your website and social media posts (team bake-offs and vivid imagery on your social profiles speak volumes).

It's easy to check an applicant's credentials and offer training where necessary but it's a lot harder to change someone's personality! If they don't share the same values as you and your team, you risk damaging the great team culture you're building.

Involving your team

Christine Mackay of award-winning animation studio Salamandra[28] told me: *"I interview based on attitude, rather than skills, because I think you can teach anybody skills to some extent, but you can't teach attitude."* She also involves her team

---

[28] *https://www.salamandra.uk/*

in the interview process: *"I think that involving everybody makes the ownership of that new person a lot more personal to the whole team."*

To some extent it's less about finding the right person for the job and more about finding a person whom your existing team will buy into. When you involve your current team in the recruitment process they're more likely to accept and give that person every possible chance. If you've successfully conveyed your work culture, purpose and values through your recruitment adverts, it's also highly unlikely your team will reject people. As empathetic leaders we value input from our existing team.

Expect flux

There is of course one more key dynamic that you need to clearly state in your adverts and interviews: Where and when do you expect people to work? The type of office format you've decided on, whether it's 9 to 5, hybrid, WFA or remote, will, for many, be the number one factor as to whether to apply for a role.

It used to be taken as read that certain job roles would require certain hours and working locations. Job specs would include location as standard and potentially an outline of a more flexible working policy if available, but generally you'd expect a role to be largely office based unless you had specifically gone looking for a remote working opportunity.

As we've already discussed, traditional office-based businesses will no longer be pigeon holed in their working format and location by industry type. Even traditional manufacturing industries may move admin and marketing roles to more remote models to save floor space and find new talent. The fact that so many people have now changed their mindset as to how and where they want to work means your decision on your culture of working hours and practices will shape the pool of candidates available to you.

The rest of your culture, the type of work you do, salary, prospects and the type of customers you work for or products you sell will, of course, also still have a huge impact on who wants to join your team. People desperate to work for you will accept going back to daily commuting and all the other hurdles of a 9 to 5 role. Similarly, those who love being physically surrounded by colleagues all day every day may accept a hybrid role if they love the rest of your culture. For many, however, the first thing they'll check is location and hours.

This potentially means a huge shift in workforce as people move to join companies that fit their ideal type of working. If you move to WFA you open up a massive pool of potential applicants that you couldn't previously have employed, but you are also now competing against a similarly wide pool of companies for the very best talent. If you stay fully office based you may limit yourselves to only certain demographics and types of people. School leavers and graduates are almost certainly still going to be drawn to a more 9 to 5, city-based culture where they can interact, socialise and learn face to face, whereas parents with families or people who want to move to more remote locations will be reluctant to join.

Will some companies end up being full of outgoing, young party-loving teams whilst others will be full of introverts who rarely venture out of their front doors? I doubt it, but there will be an interesting mixture and shift as more and more working options are available, and, regardless of which one you adopt, we must accept it will change who applies to join us.

Remember the experiment back in 2013 by Nicholas Bloom at Stanford University that I shared with you in Chapter 2? The experiment was so successful that CTrip rolled out the option to work remotely to the whole firm. Interestingly, though, they also allowed the experimental employees to reselect whether they wanted to work from home or the office.

More than half of them switched, which led to even greater gains from WFH – almost doubling to 22 per cent. Working remotely or working solely from an office is only a concept in people's minds until they experience the reality and understand how it feels for them.

Think Jam[29] is a marketing and video production agency specialising in the entertainment sector. Their website looks like the homepage of Netflix. Think of a film or TV series and they've probably worked on it. They are unique in their positioning and foothold in the industry. If you have the right skill set and want

---

[29] www.thinkjam.com

to work helping to promote some of the most recognised names and productions around then you'd want to join.

Their team page backs up the type of culture you'd expect: *"We come to work every day full of passion, commitment and unbeatable energy. We love to see our campaigns reach audiences and create smiles across the globe. Labeled the 'Jam Fam', we come together, support each other, work hard, play hard and most of all, find the fun in what we do everyday. At the heart of our culture, our wellbeing programs ensure our employee-centric environment stays that way."*

But Daniel Robey, their founder, tells me that in early 2020 he announced that the business would be WFA forever. They had offices in London, LA, New York and Birmingham but in 2015 he'd had a few beers with a friend in LA who ran a business with over 200 staff but no offices. Back then Daniel said he did the maths on a napkin and was floored by what he'd save in rent. In addition to that were the costs associated with his offices, not to mention that parking in LA has become so expensive that it has become the norm to pay for parking for staff. Daniel told me: *"You can't hire staff unless you pay for parking in LA. It costs me $300 per person, per month for parking alone. For 30 staff – you do the maths!"*

He knew his team could be just as productive following his friend's WFA model but there was one major difference: the friend had founded his business and employed people on the basis that they would work from anywhere. The people he'd hired had fully bought into and wanted to work that way. Daniel's teams had all been employed to work in offices, albeit with a very flexible working policy. On reflection, he and his leadership team decided they didn't want to risk changing their working practice retrospectively because they knew they would lose people.

Then Covid-19 hit and Daniel knew it was time to do what he knew would be right for him and for the business longer term. They'll still have hubs and still have regular meetups but the daily office has gone, and even though they work with some of the biggest brands on some of the most exciting work possible, Daniel tells me: *"We've lost a couple of great people in the last couple of months, who really want to get back into an office. And we're acutely aware that we'll probably lose a couple more. There will be people who want to sit at a desk but also there's a lot of people who welcome flexibility. I got a note from someone the other day who thanked me for allowing her flexibility and said that she's moving out of LA. Previously she said they couldn't afford to live in LA and start a family. So they've moved to another town and it's changed their economics because they're not pinned to the city. So when you talk about culture, when we look at it, from a talent perspective, or hiring perspective, I don't have to force my talent to live in the most expensive cities in the world, or near the most expensive cities in the world and pay the most expensive transport."*

The shift in individual preferences as to when and where individuals want to work going forward will continue to happen and probably quite quickly, and I believe it will be based around location and hours first and the rest of your values and culture second. We need to consider this carefully as the impact on the teams we form will be considerable.

Hire Slow

Employing people who passionately embrace the purposes and values you and your team have defined, as well as having the key skills for the role, adds an important layer to the recruitment process.

A quick hire is almost always the wrong hire because you don't know the person.

Bruce, the founder of G Adventures, is very passionate about preserving their working culture. He told me: *"We hire very slowly. Sometimes it takes us a year to hire someone who is the right fit, but it's simply not worth having the wrong fit. We're a fast-growing company; we've had double digit growth for 30 years as a business, so sometimes we have a huge need to recruit, but it's still a top priority to take our time to find the right people. It's one of the most important ingredients driving performance."*

They created a five-step recruitment process, very similar to one we use at MCM. The initial interview structure may change depending on the role, but the final interview, regardless of what position you are applying for, never changes. It's carried out by three random staff members from any of the company's staff from around the world. The staff might be managers, administrators, tour guides or any other role.

Remember the snowmobile analogy where each team member is driving themselves with you, their empathetic leader, at the front? Think of the recruitment process as a bit like this; you're all moving together as one and selecting new drivers to join the squad, rather than you barking orders or imposing a new team mate upon them.

In fact, the second-to-last interview we do at MCM is not about the role: the group of randomly picked team members who facilitate the process don't need to know any background on the individual or even need to know what role the interviewee is applying for. The process is more about whether they fit in with our values. We use a series of pre-set questions and score against these, and the score that the random group of people give a candidate determines whether they can be hired or not.

The process allows the team to score using a colour system: green, amber or red. If it's red then no matter how good that person is at their job, they simply can't be hired. The system at G Adventures is so strictly adhered to that Bruce told me of his frustration recruiting for a senior role some years ago. He'd spent 18 months recruiting for the role and finally thought he'd found someone with the right skill set. They failed the G factor culture fit interview with a red vote and he had to follow the rules.

Chapter 13

The key to the success of the process, he told me, is that: "*The panel has no idea what that person is applying for, how many years they've worked, or how many interviews they've gone through (or crucially how desperate we are as a company to fill that position). We're recruiting on personality above skill. It's taken us years to get it right; we show trust in everyone to make the right decision, and everyone who joins the company is special – they've been approved by team members and trusted to be part of our team.*"

What happens when you rush the process?

Rushing will damage your team culture and morale far faster than leaving a role empty until the perfect candidate is found. You will waste valuable time managing a bad hire.

At MCM we ask for a cover letter with every CV and won't even read a CV without one. If an applicant isn't excited enough to read our requirements and write a short summary of why they want to join us, they're not right for our team.

We also insist on a similar process, as I mentioned above, to G Adventures with a fairly lengthy minimum of five stages of interview spread over at least a month. If you are focused on finding people who are truly bought into your culture and desperate to join then they will jump through every hoop to prove they want to be a part of your team.

The five stages are:

1. 10-minute screening interview on Zoom

2. 30-minute skills and initial culture fit

3. 60-minute short presentation of skills following a written brief, then Q&A

4. Meet the team – meet a random selection of team members for a culture fit

5. Final interview

The culture interview tends to be fairly relaxed. The team generally asks about the person's background, what they do in their spare time, where they work and why they want to join. Then they have a selection of key questions they add in throughout the conversation in no particular order, which they score against on a simple one to ten.

Just like Bruce we're brave, and if they get a red light at this stage then no matter how fantastic their skills, that candidate won't be joining our team. If it's amber we have a healthy debate, and green is more or less welcome on board! We hire on the basis that if the team buys in, and you buy in, the rest is teachable and learnable (we talk more about this approach, the DiSC tool, in Chapter 15).

Some sample questions we ask include:

- What type of company culture excites you?
- How would your current team describe you?
- Do you prefer to work alone or in a team?
- Which one of our values are you most passionate about? Why?
- What mistake have you learnt the most from?
- Describe the environment in which you work best.
- How do you handle stress?
- How important is work-life balance to you?
- Do you prefer to get feedback about your performance through formal reviews or informal meetings?
- Describe your ideal boss. Ours is a bit weird!

Fire Fast

As empathetic leaders we know it's best to 'let people go', 'part company' or maybe 'consciously uncouple', but for ease of memory *Hire Slow, Fire Fast!*

Even the most stringent recruitment process might allow a bad fit to slip through, or perhaps your work culture or key team members have evolved; one or two just don't feel like a good fit anymore.

So whilst the expression is Fire Fast, that is only when every other avenue has been explored and every bit of help given to keep a team member on track. Regular one to ones, constant communication with the team and an open and honest environment will always highlight when someone is not a good fit; no matter how good their skills are, you are almost certainly damaging your team by ignoring it.

Benchmarks

If you know there are issues, do everything you can to rectify them quickly and have benchmarks as to whether change is possible. Rely on your team to help make sure your judgement isn't purely personal (they will usually be the best barometer). I've made the mistake in the past of delaying action because the individual was such a well-liked member of the team, only to find that, as liked as they were in a social setting, their work ethic was constantly in question.

When we finally made the right decision we were asked: *"Why didn't you do it sooner?"* There was no malice and the team stayed friends with the individual long after they left (as is often the case), but our work ethic, supporting the values and driving our purpose forward matters hugely to our team at MCM and they needed that support in the office as well as when out socialising.

MCM – lesson learnt

More than a decade ago we hired a brand new developer who was really nice, but there were constant problems with the standard of work (it was a complete mess the whole time). We didn't do the right thing and let them go. We did a few performance management sessions, but they were so nice we never had the heart to let them go.

They eventually left of their own accord. I met them at an event six months later and they told me they had become a school teacher. They said to me: *"I never could code very well. I didn't really understand it, and I didn't know what I was doing half the time but didn't want to admit it. I don't know why you never fired me!"*

They also told me that they would have thanked me if I'd told them that they weren't a good fit. We learnt our lesson the hard way because we endured all that pain!

A kind dismissal

As empathetic leaders it is much kinder to flag up a team misalignment. The slow agonising continuation of keeping an individual who just doesn't fit is damaging for the individual, your team and your work culture. They'll also be far happier as a person when they move on and find the people and team that's right for them!

When you let people go, leave them on a high note. Go the extra mile so they understand why they're not the best fit and support them to find the right external role for their skills, values and purpose.

You may feel like you're being a decent person by letting someone hold on but animosity quickly builds on all sides and the ending is never good.

It's about doing the right thing, feeling good about yourself as a leader and considering the feelings of that individual. If, in the future, you gain business from that or build a stronger network that's a bonus, but ultimately it's about empathy and respect.

In days gone by we'd have been told that we were being too nice, or that we weren't strong leaders, but it's come full circle. Sir Alan Sugar's famous finger pointing and "You're fired" makes for great entertainment on *The Apprentice*, but we need to put ourselves in the shoes of the people we once considered valued members of our team and recognise that they still have immense value and potential, but that they need to be in the right place.

It's false empathy to keep someone employed in a role they clearly aren't suited to or comfortable in.

Also, when people leave of their own accord to experience a new team or location, make sure they leave with your blessing and encouragement. Forcing people to stay with offers of more money or a promotion are more often than not doomed to failure. Once the decision has been made there's always going to be a nagging doubt on both sides. So let them go as friends.

Chapter 13

One of our former employees has just introduced us to a major client who has come onboard. We stayed in touch on LinkedIn. We've also just re-hired three people who used to work for us before. They left, developed some new skills and missed us so much they came back!

Chapter 13

Leadership and Listening

In Chapter 2 I said that mastering communication was one of the most essential components of leading in a non 9 to 5 working environment. Communication, trust, transparency and organisational skills are the core elements leaders need to focus on if they are to have happy and productive teams.

None of these should be new skills for leaders, but they take on a new level of importance when some or all of a team is working remotely.

So, let's finish by looking at how we build trust and how we communicate perfectly across the entire team; both of these are skills that need a huge injection of empathy.

Part 4

More Remote, More Trust and a Thriving Culture?

One of the major concerns team leaders and business owners still seem to have over anything less than a return to the old way of being in anything other than a traditional 9 to 5 office routine is the loss of their culture.

Culture, as we've already seen, is far more than slogans on walls and physically being in the same place every day. It is far more reliant on a cohesive team that is open, honest and complements each other's skill sets. A team that is not so similar and close that no debate or competition exists, but is aligned along a common goal and full trusting of each other.

Supporting this and ensuring the culture thrives has to be trust and honesty right from the top of the team: from you, the leader. So if anything, working outside the 9 to 5 structure means we have no choice but to place more trust in our teams and to help them to grow and work together without constant supervision. By enabling a team to learn more about each other, encouraging them to give and to want to receive the trust of those around them, you will see a large amount of the culture building is done for you.

Alongside some team building exercises and principles that we'll talk about in this chapter, and possibly the biggest link to make all of this work, is COMMUNICATION.

Learning how to communicate in a structured yet natural way, with not too much interference but just the right level of support, is a skill set we're all learning to adopt and fine tune. The holy grail is a perfect blend of face to face, video, email, texts, Slacks, groups or whatever combination of real and virtual that you find works for your team.

Developing Empathy Within Your Team

There are many traditionally accepted factors that motivate individuals within a team. These include money, status, belonging, learning, praise, pride and trust, but now there are additional elements to consider around where and when we are expected to work. If you go from 9 to 5 to fully remote with an established team then you won't be pleasing everyone. If you start hiring as a WFA company then you will attract people who want an extremely flexible working environment.

As a startup hiring your first employees in line with your working policy, values and purposes you at least know you are attracting people who want to live all three of those traits. However, as an established business, whichever route you go there will be some who wished you'd gone a different route.

As we've already discussed, there will be some who simply need and want the benefits 9 to 5 brings them, but most will want more freedom than before and the team will not be together as often as they used to be. This is why understanding your team as individuals, and having them understand themselves and their team members, is crucial to building a truly functional team.

In American business consultant and author Patrick Lencioni's book *The Five Dysfunctions of a Team*[30] (I highly recommend the manga comic version!), he explains that trust is the foundation of every effective team and the leader is crucial to building that trust. In a working model where people work from anywhere, that trust becomes even more imperative.

---

[30] *Patrick M. Lencioni, (2002), The Five Dysfunctions of a Team: A Leadership Fable,* John Wiley & Sons

Why is trust so important?

When **trust** exists, then healthy **conflict** and debate can occur. Conflict, he argues, is crucial for teams to remain agile and collaborative. Teams that become too friendly tend to stop conflict for fear of offending each other. At the other extreme, a team that becomes too fractured will have constant debate (in cliques and whispers) between meetings, which erodes the heart of the team.

Commitment to follow through on a group decision becomes possible within a functional team because you've had your voice heard, listened to the other arguments and trust the majority decision. This means the whole team can make progress. You also understand that reaching a decision is better than not reaching one at all, even if it isn't the one you want. There's nothing worse than a few team members who feel they have no say in a decision, have not heard the reasoning, turn against the idea and have no commitment to helping it succeed. If you've watched *The Apprentice* you'll have seen this sort of mutiny a million times! The simple inclusion from your trusted team members is often enough for you to feel you're valued and heard and sway you to support rather than turn against.

Accountability is key to ensuring team members will hold each other accountable for their part of the plan or decision rather than always having to be the micromanaging leader. Having sufficient trust in each other and full buy-in for team decisions means your team will feel empowered to hold one another accountable without fear of upsetting each other (or causing trouble!).

Excellent **results** then follow because there is mutual trust, which means healthy debate and confrontations are fair and not feared. This brings joint commitment to plans for which the team, rather than just you, hold each other accountable and help each other to achieve.

Trust, as we know, is the base of the pyramid from which all other areas of team effectiveness stem. It is potentially harder to nurture outside of the 9 to 5 office structure when we can't see what others are doing all day every day, but if the work contributions remain high and delivered to deadline, trust will build over time.

Owning up to mistakes builds trust

A large degree of trust is earned through demonstrating vulnerabilities and admitting to mistakes. Opening up about personal lives, preferences and challenges also breaks down barriers and reinforces trust and support in one another. Some of this may happen naturally in an office environment; much more happens outside the office at informal lunches, walks or drinks after work. Much of it, however, can be strengthened and honed by some simple team sharing exercises that can be carried out whether you are remote or face to face.

DiSC profiles and personal assessment tools

If you haven't experienced DiSC®[31], or any of the variations of these tools before, then carrying out an assessment for each of

---

[31] *https://www.discprofile.com/*

your team members, including yourself, gives an insightful and astonishingly accurate insight into your and your team members' key strengths and weaknesses. It also throws a spotlight on individual personalities and approaches to life.

DiSC® is described as a behaviour self-assessment tool and was originally based on the 1928 emotional and behavioural theory of psychologist William Moulton Marston, which centres on four personality traits:

D for dominance

People who place emphasis on immediate results, taking action and challenging.

I for influence

More open personalities who place an emphasis on expressing enthusiasm, taking action and encouraging collaboration.

S for steadiness

Dependable profiles who place emphasis on supporting, keeping stability and enjoying collaboration.

C for compliance

Where a key focus is on quality, accuracy, expertise, keeping stability and challenging assumptions.

There are now a variety of companies that offer access to versions of this tool. I highly recommend Everything DiSC®[32] via Rachel Boothroyd[33], which bases their model on Marston's theories, and further splits each personality type down as illustrated below:

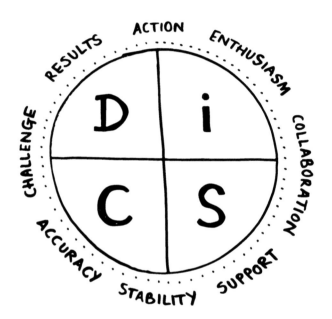

---

[32] www.everythingdisc.com

[33] www.rachelboothroyd.com

Is your weakness a strength?

Whilst the concept of profiling may sound intrusive, or a little too much like detective work, it is far from it. It helps individuals understand that what they may have thought of as a weakness could be a strength.

It shows where they may share key common traits and goals with team members who they thought had opposing personalities.

It also helps because:
- You learn how best to approach each team member (their preference)
- You find out why certain people are quiet in meetings yet highly productive and creative outside of them
- It allows team members to empathise more with each other
- It contributes to the functioning of a team by highlighting vulnerabilities and facilitating communication and conversation.

The best teams are full of variety

The best teams are made up of a mixture of personality types that bring a wide range of abilities and expertise together. A team that is made up of all the same personality types will not have lively or productive debates, and, whilst they may have a friendly and happy culture, it is unlikely to bring fantastic results. A DiSC® assessment can therefore always help identify personality types you may be missing, and help you to look out for these in future applicants.

Platforms such as *Everything DiSC®* are simple to use and quick to complete. They also give the ability for team members to compare their results against others' in real time, which, in itself, can spark lively debate.

Profiles are generally colour-coded and can then be split further into distinct areas within each of the profiles as shown earlier in the chapter. Other companies, such as *Insights*, use slightly different versions with Insights Discovery[34] basing theirs on the theory of personality outlined by Swiss psychologist Carl Gustav Jung in 1921. Instead of DiSC®, theirs defines personality types as cool blue, fiery red, earth green and sunshine yellow.

How the empathetic leader has evolved

Interestingly, the team leader of old would nearly always sit heavily in the D section of these profile charts or the fiery red section. The leaders of the future, and especially the leader of non 9 to 5 office-based teams will, it is predicted, sit far more often in the I to S sections (or somewhere between earth green and sunshine yellow) where empathy, support and listening are the key traits.

As with any exercises like this, it's key that they aren't simply carried out then filed away. With a full team DiSC® session you will find people keep commenting back on the session and explaining their actions or the actions of others by their DiSC® type.

It might be used in defensive humour! *"Oh that'll be because I'm a DiSC® yellow!"* Or, it might be used as a way to explain why they feel uncomfortable with a situation, or why they are

---

[34] https://www.insights.com/products/insights-discovery/

disagreeing with a suggestion. The DiSC® profiles tend to go beyond an appraisal and it's useful to revisit and update them whenever someone new joins the team or if the team needs some fine-tuning or stimulation!

The personality manual

Emily Cason, who manages the marketing team for the charity Cats Protection[35], showed me an equally valuable personality tool. Emily was growing her team and building a WFA culture long before 2020. Having recently recruited in the 2020 lockdown, she had five or six team members she hadn't met face to face yet. Whilst their regular team meetings, plus a Monday morning general team chat about the weekend and a Friday wind-down quiz, had enabled the team to get to know each other well, Emily also introduced a *user manual* for the whole team.

Quite simply, each team member has to complete their own *How to Work With Me* manual.

This includes:

- Their likes
- Their background
- Whether they are a morning person or a night owl
- When they are able to be at their most productive
- Their communication style and preferred method of communication
- What they do that people may misinterpret
- Strengths and weaknesses.

---

[35] www.cats.org.uk

Their answers are shared with all team members, not just as a bit of fun to break down some of those virtual barriers, but also so team members really get to understand and respect each other. Emily told me that if she says, "*I'm most productive when I only check my emails twice a day*", people won't be offended if she doesn't reply immediately.

The user manual needn't be long, complicated or feel uncomfortable or phony to complete. It should be explained that it's a guide to how you like to work and be interacted with and that not every preference and suggestion will be met! In some way it should also be tailored around your values and purpose statements. But, at its centre, it's a series of basic questions such as:

How would people describe your communication style? How do you like to communicate best: email, phone, face to face?

I'm better at communicating first in writing then a face-to-face chat. I can be clearer and more concise without too much waffle in an email but would always like to chat through things so nothing is misunderstood.

What do you do that people may misunderstand? Where have you been misunderstood in the past due to your mannerisms, quirks or communication style?

People say my cross face and my thinking face are very similar so apparently it's hard to know which one I'm wearing. (Many thanks to Lucy at Haymarket Group for this real life example!)

What is your key strength? What do you enjoy being best at and how can you help the team learn this?

I'm highly organised and love to make plans. I love sharing all the tools and tips I've learnt over the years and helping people implement them. It's great when I hear people say "I've eaten that frog today" and knowing I shared that tip with them.

What's your biggest weakness and what do you need to get better at?

Over planning. Sometimes I get too wrapped up in the planning to stop and celebrate the results.

What time of day do you feel your work is most productive?

I'm a morning person. If I get uninterrupted time for the first quarter of the day, I'm much more productive than stopping and starting, and by 4pm I'm best just checking emails.

As always, these questions can't be completed and then just filed away. They should be shared and discussed regularly and be revisited and revised at quarterly meetups. They can be used as a great tool to help each other grow and develop by sharing feedback and suggestions as you get to know each other more fully. When shared with new team members when they join, they can also act as a great onboarding tool for a new member to get a sense of the diversity of the team from day one.

Chapter 15

Understanding increases trust

Whatever methods you use, the more your team understands each other then the more they'll trust each other. It is all too easy to misunderstand someone's mannerisms or mood. How often have you read something into an email that the sender did not intend? If someone is more comfortable expressing their ideas one to one and doesn't open up fully in a group debate, that doesn't mean they don't have great ideas or a valuable contribution to make. If you each understand and accept this up front, you help draw the best from each other.

As author Patrick Lencioni said in The Five Dysfunctions of a Team[36]: *"Teamwork remains the ultimate competitive advantage, both because it is so powerful and so rare. If you could get all the people in an organisation rowing in the same direction, you could dominate any industry, in any market, against any competition, at any time."*

However, understanding each other is just the beginning. To grow and develop that understanding, to facilitate healthy conflict, to grow commitment, accountability and ultimately results, you need to master possibly the most difficult challenge of the non 9 to 5 office world, and that is communication.

---

[36] *Patrick M. Lencioni, (2002), The Five Dysfunctions of a Team: A Leadership Fable, John Wiley & Sons*

Communicating in the
Non 9 to 5 Office

Zoom, Teams, Slack, email, social media and all the other channels available to us are incredible tools to keep in constant touch with our teams. They make remote working so much easier. However, quality technology can only take us so far: it's the quality of our communication that counts.

Having set up MCM in our spare room in the '90s, we were early adopters of Microsoft NetMeeting: one of the first voice over internet protocol systems (VoIP), which meant we could talk to each other via a headset and microphone rather than the phone.

Because internet access was via a modem (that sounded like a kettle boiling), it had to reconnect every time using the phone line; technically we were using the phone! Back then, the internet was also charged by the minute and I always had to remind my first employee to disconnect after a call or he'd rack up huge phone bills for MCM.

Chapter 16

The speed at which technology has progressed is staggering and before 2020 none of the companies were harnessing even a fraction of the power of Zoom or its companions.

Whilst we can rely on their capabilities, we must now finetune our own communication through:

- Planning
- Scheduling
- Maintaining our communication loops

Communication needs to be planned and scheduled yet also remain open and unscripted. We need to replicate the good parts of face to face with just enough humanity and personality without drifting too far into meaningless noise or soulless instruction.

The key areas we need to get right are split into four distinct categories:

- Leader to team
- Leader to individual
- Team to team
- Team building (remote)

And lastly, the glue that every company I spoke to needed in some shape or form (whether it be monthly, quarterly or annually):

- Team building (face to face)

Chapter 16

Leader to team

When you see people in the flesh every day it's easy to speak to everyone all at once and even go round saying a quick hello to every immediate team member. Some of the best leaders throughout history are known for being seen on the shop floor, getting a feel for the temperature, for the pain points and concerns and generally being there to roll their sleeves up and show they're happy to get their hands dirty.

Keeping this consistent fully remotely or when you are face to face only a few days a week takes far more planning, effort and ultimately time from a leader. It's easy to assume everyone knows the direction of the business, for instance, when you're always face to face and in earshot, but that has often proved not to be the case. As you move from meeting to meeting and idea to idea it's easy to not completely communicate everything all of the time. The risk of doing this when remote is even greater.

The assumption that we just need to use Zoom more and replicate what we had in an office is not the answer. By the nature of remote, WFA and especially a hybrid working pattern, communication becomes an art that needs to be relearnt and redefined.

Graeme Newton who heads the marketing team at the huge global charity World Vision told me: *"When I joined World Vision back in about 2006 in New Zealand I was working in* a hybrid virtual space. I had a team of about 20 staff, some an hour's flight away from head office. It worked really well because they had the technology in place to have a really great conference facility so all the tech was in place and that's part of it, but the other part is actually that, even back then, they trained managers to work really effectively with remote teams.

"You learned that you could be in a room and an office with a group of people and then one or two at home and it's almost impossible for them to enter the conversation because all the centre of the conversation is based around those in the room. As a manager, I was taught to think a lot more broadly than just who's in the room. How do I engage those who are online? How do I bring them into the conversation? How do we make sure their voices are heard? And that really kind of inclusive management approach was important for genuine hybrid working and is just as much so today.

"Today, based in the UK with staff around the world, I find I've gotten a really good rhythm with my teams. We've used a few different things. I have structured one-to-one meetings with my team, both with teams and also with individual staff. All of this does take more effort but it's that idea of being a multiplying leader: how can you multiply your output by investing in your team and seeing them grow and develop? So from my perspective, it's about investment. It's not about you spending time: it's about investing time and the things which will multiply the results the most."

Not only do we need to invest in our teams by taking the lead with communication, but we also need to help them develop the habit of remote communication. Arguably it is the hybrid model that causes the most challenges here. As Graeme said, it is always a challenge when some are in the room with you and others are remote. No matter how good technology may be, it is easier to communicate with people who are in the same room as you. That millisecond time lag that confuses our brains on Zoom and the simple fact we're much more used to making eye contact with people directly means it's easy for external members to feel excluded. That is until, of course, as one person told me, "with the current speed of change, in the not too distant future we'll be sitting around a boardroom table again in a full team meeting but we won't know which attendees are really there and which are holograms!". (Maybe pour them a glass of water and see what happens? Surely it can't get that good?)

When it comes to leader-to-team communication, there are a number of elements it's important to consider.

Location

If you have full team meetings then the easiest way is to insist, where possible, those happen on face-to-face days or fully remote days. Give people the choice then it's quite likely the ones who come to the office are the more dominant DiSC types and the ones at home, the less vocal S and C types. If you attend the meeting in person you also create the insecurity that those who are there in the flesh with you will be favoured long term over those who are remote.

Structure is therefore essential for full team meetings. No matter how liberal we are with people's working hours, place of work and trust in them that they will simply get the job done in their own time, people still need and want structure and guidance in key areas of their working life. Team meetings should be planned and made a regular habit. By habit this doesn't just mean a time of day but also how the meetings are attended and conducted.

As a WFA business that has clearly laid out that only monthly, quarterly and annual meetings will be face to face then this needs to be the norm. If you have several team members who choose to be in an office space together when some of those meetings are happening then that's fine, but try not to be in the same room with them if you're there too! At least try to be on a separate screen. As small a concession as this may be, it is small perceptions such as you being in the same room regularly with the same small group of people when the rest are remote that can quietly breed discontent and erode the trust you've worked hard to build.

With a hybrid model, that challenge multiplies so your key team meetings should be on face-to-face days, which means that having a fully flexible attendance policy of choosing your three days working in the office doesn't work well. You need to establish core days when everyone must attend the office as the norm otherwise you run an even higher risk of team divisions and cliques forming. If you're relaxing to a hybrid model from 9 to 5 then setting key days when people need to be in the office shouldn't be a problem, but human nature says flexibility needs to be flexed as hard as possible! Without setting boundaries you'll soon have plenty more admin and HR issues to contend with as people argue over which days suit them best to be in the office.

Structure

Even if you've created flexibility in working locations it's important to adhere to a structure for meetings. Staff feel more secure when they know what to expect from meetings.

Cameras on

If you were happy in the face-to-face 9 to 5 world with people phoning into a meeting from the hallway rather than sitting at the table with the rest of you then go ahead and allow cameras off. Otherwise, there should no longer be any reason for cameras off. If people are happy working from home then it is important you know they have a suitable space to work in that is conducive to the type of work you produce as a team. If they're not happy or don't have the space to work from home then you need to provide them with space in a suitable space: that could be your office, a shared workspace or place of their choice. Even as a last resort they can add a photo background,

Chapter 16

if you don't mind half their head disappearing through the meeting, but cameras should always be on unless there is a really good reason. That reason – perhaps they're in a location with poor reception, en route to a meeting or away from home – must be a temporary reason and not regularly repeated.

This isn't a big brother move and you need to explain the reasoning to your team. Most will naturally understand that it just feels rude if everyone else can see and wave at each other and one is a faceless voice. Those who don't agree need to understand that, even when working remotely, a small part of communication still involves body language.

Add to that the trust you are trying to foster between your team members. If someone's camera is off then naturally people will be questioning why. Most teams have always had that one individual who screeches to a sliding halt as they arrive at a face-to-face meeting with seconds to spare, shirt buttons misaligned and hair unkempt on a fairly regular basis. These same individuals will leave themselves seconds to spare when attending a virtual meeting, but instead of having time to wake up in some way on the train on the way in, the natural suspicion will be whether they have woken up seconds ago.

The team needs everyone to be prepared, at peak performance and ready to contribute, so regardless of whether the screen is off through a temperamental laptop camera, poor time keeping, sloppy dressing, juggling child care, a hangover or whatever multitude of reasons there could be, the camera being off needs addressing. This is best done one to one just as you would with the repeat offender who arrives late face to face. There has to be a reason and you can usually help resolve that reason. If their laptop really is faulty then get it checked and replaced. Time keeping and productivity courses and even "how to conduct your-self on a Zoom call" are plentiful. A simple chat and guidance from you may be all it needs. All the things you'd naturally do face to face need to be addressed in just the same way. Leaving the 'camera off' issue unresolved, however, is simply not an option.

How you communicate

As human beings we rely on body language more than we realise. Obviously, working remotely we can still see the person on screen but it's not yet our natural environment.

There will be times when:

- We feel self conscious because we're faced with our own reflection
- We fold our arms – but we'd never do this in person because it feels defensive in the presence of another
- We slouch (to be at the right angle for the camera)
- We speak loudly or quietly because of what's going on in our own environment
- We frown or grimace (because there's a screen in our face or notifications keep popping up)
- We have technology problems which cause us to get frustrated
- We're on mute but just made our best point ever!

Chapter 16

Make your words count

In team meetings, and any meetings with your team members, the words you speak now matter even more than they did in the past. Planning what you need to say, who you need to praise, what developments are on the horizon and what success looks like this week is important as all need to be communicated with precision.

You need to be far more aware of how your words may be interpreted and whether they'll be fully taken on board.

With a digital presence you need to consider how your words could be interpreted because you don't have the 'atmosphere' or the full body language to rely on. When you're standing in front of your team, you can quickly take in expressions and gauge reactions. You pick up quickly on whether your words are being understood and how they're being interpreted as you unconsciously scan the faces in front of you.

Granted, you can often get that wrong even face to face. I can think of plenty of team meetings in the past where I've built up the announcements and great news, excitedly visualising that scene from The Wolf of Wall Street where everyone stands and beats their chests, united in excited chanting, only to be greeted by unreadable expressions. Much later, I'd be told individually how excited everyone was and how everyone was talking about what I'd said when they left the room. "Dear Team, if you read this bit – I want chest beating and chanting in future, please!"

Scanning every face and every expression on a Zoom screen continuously is virtually impossible. Your words alone need to convey your message and you need to encourage your team to communicate back verbally by explaining that you can't read their reactions and nor can their colleagues. If you don't have a great culture of encouraging team-to-team communication, they won't have that moment where they leave the room and share their excitement. They'll feel they were the only one excited and the feeling will soon be lost.

Stuart Miles, founder of one of the longest running tech news sites, www.Pocket-Lint.com, has run his team remotely since starting the business in 2003. He told me: *"I've always been conscious of the fact that the lack of non-verbal communication means you are better off over communicating and that the team learns to do the same. You don't have that moment where you're leaving the office to get a sandwich or something and you can have a spur of the moment chat with a team member or a colleague to gauge their feelings or reactions. The informal conversation where someone says: 'I just want to tell you that you're doing this, and it's not ideal or it's winding people up' just doesn't happen. So as a leader you have to encourage communication that makes sure things don't fester and brood. Be seen to make that call, have an honest chat, discuss and debate. But you have to arrange to do it because that natural moment rarely comes."*

So, as an empathetic leader, you have to encourage communication that prevents issues from festering. Be proactive because that natural moment won't arise.

Delivery

Regular team meetings and updates are essential but they don't have to only be when everyone is together. They also don't all have to be virtual or even live. Provided you have a schedule for key meetings and updates, then exploring other ways of communicating can help ensure your messages never get lost. We need to strike a balance between communication overload and utilising so many channels that people are dragged down social media or email rabbit holes.

Face-to-face delivery still can't be beaten and, as we'll hear later, it still very much has a place in the WFA model, whether it's monthly, quarterly or less often. These meetings should be treated as the gold dust meetings, focusing on team interaction and collaboration rather than too many broadcast messages.

Daily and weekly full team Zoom updates and meetings delivered effectively, consistently, concisely and with clear messaging come next, but how often is it that every team member is present at every meeting? There's nearly always someone on holiday or at an essential external meeting so key messages can easily be repeated in other formats. In fact, one suggestion is to record your core team meetings and have them available for catch up or run them through a tool such as www.otter.ai that transcribes the video to a pretty decent written script that can be quickly skim read or can have key points highlighted.

Where Slack and Teams are great conversation channels, email still has its place in delivering messages that don't need instant reading. It's more formal and allows team members to read non-urgent messages at a time that's best for them. If you've taught them the 'turn off email' lessons then they'll only read these when they're in full receptive mode!

For less formal keep-in-touch messages, which also move across into the team-to-team territory, consider a team WhatsApp channel. This can be a great and more informal way of communicating but comes with all the social media caveats. Overuse and too many team members posting memes means that at best your message is lost and at worst you cause yet more social media overload that stretches into people's weekends. The latter isn't necessarily a bad thing and often happens on our main WhatsApp group but the key is it's never abused and over done. It's usually funny at the weekend or someone seeing a great campaign idea somewhere and the key is there's no pressure on anyone to respond. Join in if you like, view only or totally ignore – nobody passes judgement.

A great leader-to-team communication method that straddles both formal and informal is a brief weekly video message. It can be a round up of key events, new business, developments etc or an informal round up of your own personal week, or a mixture of both.

Louise at www.kyero.com and her husband each broadcast a five-minute video to their team on a Friday. Louise said: "It's just a way for us to connect with the team. This week, I read a book called Chatter by Ethan Crass, so I shared his *ideas around how you can use the voice in your head to your advantage or turn it off."*

Online communication can be informal and effective: press record, direct phone at face, talk, press stop then send. In fact, often the rougher around the edges it is, the better received it will be. This is about you connecting with your team with honesty, authenticity, vulnerability and empathy. Show them you're human with the same range of emotions as them.

Lucy at Haymarket Group told me: *"I find that I make more time in my calendar to talk to my team. We have task-driven meetings, and there are team social sessions and softer chats. When we were always in the office you'd just turn around and have a chat, whereas now it all has to be scheduled in, which is a bit like planning the fun, but it's important because otherwise it won't happen."*

Leader to individual

Structured or unstructured, your team members need to hear from you on a one-to-one basis. Some of your team may work with you on a more regular basis than others and when you're not face to face it's easy to find some team members rarely get to interact with you directly. In an office you'll wander around and even a nod and a smile in the right direction is all someone needs for them to know you know they exist.

As marketing director Robert Stead admitted: *"Remotely, it's very easy to find you haven't spoken to somebody for a week because they've just not been on your radar for whatever reason. So I do think that's going to put more pressure on team leaders to be really organised."*

As forced as it may sound, several people I spoke to recommended keeping a list of all team members and noting how often you speak to them. That doesn't mean you have to schedule necessarily, but it does help you see who may be getting less attention.

The following are some suggestions for how you can ensure you get the right level of interaction between your team on a one-to-one basis, even when you're WFA or adopting a hybrid model.

How are you?

Remember the telephone? That impromptu phone call is welcomed. No video, no agenda, just a brief, "Hello, how are you?" once in a while can really boost someone's day far more than you may expect.

Alternatively, allocate a time when people can drop in to talk to you without an agenda. Gerhard Forie, Marketing Director at Aston Martin, told me he had been working hybrid or remotely for many years based in South Africa, Japan and the UK when he was at Nissan Motor company. With teams based in many different locations he had a drop-in session several times a week where anyone knew they could join an open video session and ask him anything they liked. It was on a first come, first served basis. Sometimes he said he'd have a queue and sometimes he'd have nobody, but it was just the fact that he was available that was appreciated more than anything.

One to ones

Another great way to stay in touch on a regular basis are monthly one to ones. The appraisal system of old that was repeated on an annual basis found a few good points then focused on what you should improve on, set some targets and then went back in a file for a year. This simply won't work in the WFA world.

I remember having appraisals when I first worked in the city. We had to handwrite our answers to a whole series of questions then give the form to our manager. They were linked to pay reviews and whispers used to spread across the office floor of when they were starting, who'd been seen, who hadn't and how good or bad they were. They were a nerve racking ordeal with, in my experience, little outcome.

The ironic appraisal

I vividly remember one appraisal where my boss told a colleague and I that we should cut down the length of our client lunches (which were hugely encouraged at the time) so we could focus on getting some mundane office tasks completed over the next few weeks. This was all duly recorded on the form and the form duly signed and filed in his desk drawer. He then took me and said colleague to the pub for a post-appraisal lunch that lasted until evening! We still laugh about it to this day when we talk and I have a feeling the office tasks were probably never completed and the appraisal was certainly not taken out of that drawer until the following April!

Mentorship tools

At MCM we use a system of one to ones that we class more as a mentorship tool. Each team member privately sets themselves one big hairy goal (BHG) for the next 12 months. That goal has to be achievable but not easy to achieve. It needs to push them out of their comfort zone and be in some way related to their career, but crucially has to be something that fills them with a sense of pride and has them grinning from ear to ear when they think about achieving it.

They also have to set themselves a quarterly goal which is easier and more achievable and may serve as a building block to help them on the path to the BHG. Both these put the development path directly in the individual's hands. Often they come with several possible goals and ask for help deciding which will benefit both them and the team most.

We then work together to break down the goals into achievable steps and decide on mentoring partners to help at varying stages of the journey. This may be people who have specific skills in the areas the individual wants to develop or simply people they respect and feel comfortable being challenged and inspired by. It doesn't have to be the same person throughout the goal journey; different stages may need different input and it means the entire team gets to share skills and help each other. In doing so, they often uncover skills they share that they didn't realise they had.

Whilst everyone is always aiming to achieve their goals, we heavily emphasise that not hitting them isn't failure. Every step is more of a step than we would have had without the goal process. So if we only get half way or we change direction along the way it doesn't matter. What's crucial is you always have support if you get stuck, lose momentum or feel you want to give up.

As a leader, once this process is shared and underway, you then schedule to mentor particular team members depending on your skills and their goals, or simply join monthly sessions as you're needed or on a quarterly basis.

The process gives a clear and achievable path to help team members develop, keeps you or one of your managers in a regular feedback and collaboration loop with the individual and, most importantly, empowers the individual to own and develop their own sense of purpose and fulfilment.

Team to team and remote team building

Many people I talk to about non 9 to 5 talk about the importance of recreating the "water cooler" effect. Whether it was actually at the water cooler, in the kitchen, in the games room or on the way to lunch, most natural and collaborative conversations happened away from the office desk.

This is good news for remote working as the desk had actually become a closely guarded domain that was there for working at. Very often in our and many other offices, people at desks would have headphones on to block out interruptions. Then they'd take them off, wander off to the "water cooler" and BOOM the conversation would flow. Well, sort of, and maybe not every time but in general conversations were away from desks and collaboration was in meeting rooms.

Meeting rooms are easy to recreate on Zoom and can be a great deal more time efficient. Regular team meetings can and should be scheduled for daily short briefings and regular weekly updates. In an ideal WFA world immediate team members such as a leadership team, design team, event team etc should meet up monthly face to face if possible and, if location allows, then more regularly if needed. WFA does not mean no more face to face and no more human interaction.

Without face-to-face interaction, are we doomed?

I've read many articles and heard talks that are anti-WFA because: *"We are humans and humans were designed to interact. Without interaction and social contact we are all doomed."* A quick Google of whether this is true or not reveals: *"As humans, social interaction is essential to every aspect of our health. Research shows that having a strong network of support or strong community bonds fosters both emotional and physical health and is an important component of adult life."*[37]

So there you go: a university in Georgia confirms that we need social interaction. We all know it's true. The vast majority of us do enjoy and feed off social interaction. Some love being with huge groups of people continuously; others, smaller, closer groups or family and many, a happy medium. We need people to talk to and share ideas, experiences and problems with. We feed off each other's knowledge and enjoy good healthy debates, displays of emotion and, above, all laughter and fun.

Inspired by the new

Not working at a desk in an office from 9 to 5 five days a week doesn't mean we no longer have quality social interaction. We may have to plan how, when and with whom we interact a little more, but don't we do that socially anyway?

---

[37] *South University, (2018), "Why Being Social is Good for You", 1 May*

2020 was unique in that people were working from home and also weren't allowed to mix with others for a good proportion of time. In normal times you get to choose when and where you see and interact with people, be that face to face, by phone, screen or any other means.

WFA does not mean do not meet face to face; it means we need to get the balance right and maybe do a little more planning. Planning that may, if we're honest, cut out some of that social interaction we didn't benefit from in the past!

It's easy to hire a meeting space by the hour now almost anywhere in the world. There are also plenty of restaurants, coffee shops and even homes and gardens that WFA teams have regularly been meeting in for years. They leave their desks and meet, collaborate, interact, bond and generally enjoy each other's company. Then they go back to their desks to work. The regularity will depend on the locations your teams work in. Many have talked of hubs forming naturally in different areas and different cities for impromptu meetups and collaboration. Face to face does not disappear with WFA. You just need to more consciously schedule the more regular meetups.

Commuting to the same office has benefits in terms of routine, comfort and security, whereas travelling to different locations, sharing experiences, meals and drinks then returning to the comfort of your home or outsourced desk space, in my mind, has far greater potential to stimulate relationships, collaboration and constant inspiration.

Chapter 16

The following are some of the team-to-team communications to encourage in a remote, WFA or hybrid working world.

Full team meetups

Our quarterly full team meeting days start with reflections on the past quarter, updates, individual presentations and a collaborative debate as to how we can be at our best for the next quarter. We've held them in a barn, surrounded by fields and trees with a barbecue lunch, with the afternoon spent quad biking and generally socialising. We've then done the same format in a conference room on the 24th floor of the Shard followed by an afternoon food tour and an evening of drinks.

We have future meetings set for a venue by the sea on the South coast, Shoreditch and back to our roots in Tonbridge. The time between these meetings flies by and the team bonding and collaboration does not disappear the minute we leave a venue. Every time we meet we continue to strengthen those bonds.

Maintaining team-to-team communication remotely

In between these meetings is where the challenge lies. For many people, this is far less natural than the type of conversation that happens spontaneously face to face. In offices, we're encouraged to communicate but idle chatter may be frowned upon. We want people to be sociable and build relationships but not waste their days chatting about Netflix or where they went last night. That balance is often hard to find and is one of the prime reasons people in open-plan offices can often be seen wearing headphones. I know several people who have admitted they can't work listening to music but put headphones on as a signal to others not to disturb them.

Outside of the office you want to make sure people are communicating so that those away days and the face-to-face time is built upon continuously. You need people to be communicating not just so they collaborate on their work, which is easier and can be more scheduled, but also to build those relationships, trust and avoid potential isolation feelings.

Encouraging and replicating "good mornings", "goodbyes", chat and non-lead interaction has to be an important part of your culture. As a 9 to 5 moving to a WFA or even hybrid model this can seem an initial challenge. Telling people to chat more is not natural. You can't force chat and shouldn't need to, and you don't want to grow a culture where productivity falls off a cliff because chat takes over. You can, however, encourage and remove any taboo from non-work remote conversation so it becomes an accepted part of your culture.

Those businesses I spoke to who have been WFA for many years found it surprising that many companies were finding the transition such a challenge. Most use Slack or Teams as conversation platforms and have multiple channels. In fact, Dale Davies of Exposure Ninja, who employ over 120 people and have been fully remote for over eight years at the time of writing, told me they have over 50 channels active at any one time. Those channels that don't get used often are replaced with new ones or merged so it is always fresh, and the majority are used regularly. "*It is a fully embedded and natural part of our culture,*" he told me. "*We don't have to force conversation and not everyone joins in but the majority do on a daily basis.*"

I asked Dale if they had had issues with people spending too much time chatting or productivity amongst certain individuals dropping from overuse. He thought long and hard and said he did remember one time, several years ago, where they had to have a chat with a small group to be careful it didn't take over. But it was minor and only once in all that time. He also told me, as several others have, that the most contributed to and most active channel is... "Food Porn" and has been for several years. Just in case you're stuck for channel ideas!

Office banter

The office banter has become totally natural to many teams via these remote channels, and just as they would be face to face, these are often easily linked to team building and work-related events. Louise from Kyero told me: "*There's constant banter. It's relevant and human. We generally all say good morning and goodbye. We have a wide range of channels on Slack including one called a 'jar of awesome' where you can share amazing things that have happened to you or to the company. It might be a sales target that's been hit; it might be a traffic number that's been hit. Or it might be 'my little boy passed his exam' or something. It's a way of sharing and celebrating together.*"

Other examples of channels they have are a "Thank you" channel, so everyone can thank whoever they want to, again, for the smallest or largest thing, a "lounge", a "Random" channel and of course a "Food Porn" channel, which is used for everything from a photo of a great meal in a restaurant to a cake someone's baked.

In the companies that I spoke to, this way of sharing is personal choice. People don't have to say goodbye and they don't have to comment on all of the posts. It's there to use as you see fit. Some days people will be more active than others. The way you're feeling and your workload will influence how much you interact, just like they do in the face-to-face world.

There should never be a sense of people feeling they ought to respond to all of the posts. It's a support. It's not an obligation. But if you gradually make it part of your culture, you will find most people take part in some way.

It may just be responding to a good morning with a wave, but most companies find interaction soon gathers pace and if you have your team culture, purpose, values and trust fully embedded then you never need to worry about misuse.

Tamara at The Social Element told me they have a chat room where people share emerging social memes. It's crucial that they keep their finger on the pulse for their clients."*We're constantly asking, 'have you seen the latest Cuthbert Caterpillar thing?' or whatever it may be. So we're spotting what's going on as part* of our service, but the conversation within that space is hilarious. There's plenty of work chat but alongside that there's also just sort of random chat. Just as there would be in person."

With team members in multiple time zones, Tamara says many people come straight to the chanels to get their social hit for the day (there'll be a flurry of activity as her teams in America wake up).

The key to helping keep this conversation alive is to try new things whilst keeping what's working fresh. In a digital environment we need to facilitate conversation more by planning and nudging this communication along. Tamara says: "We experiment, and if it doesn't work, move on. For instance, we just started some employee resource groups, which is more around a group for parents in the company and an LGBTQ group as well. We also do things like photo competitions. I mean, it sounds so simple, but we're just getting people to be part of something. So those communities, I think, foster a huge sense of connection."

There are plenty of tools available to help spur on one-to-one team conversations outside of the chanels too. You can have a team video meeting and then use break out rooms using a random breakout facility or use something like https://coffee-roulette.com/ that emails randomly paired team members once a week suggesting they book a 15-minute virtual coffee break.

Team building (face to face)

Regardless of how successful your virtual team activities are, keeping some kind of regular face-to-face meeting to bond your team and keep those relationships alive is crucial to most businesses. Whether you include presentations, updates and collaboration sessions is optional. Some with; some without. But external team events tend to be something that people appreciate and remember for years to come. The investment in time, effort and cash is far wider reaching than just the one-day event.

In the late '80s city days I can still vividly remember our team events. Our culture of work hard, play hard was regularly enhanced by the 20 or so of us in the core team meeting away from the city at a team event. That might be a spa hotel followed by dinner and drinks, a golf day followed by dinner and drinks, a day at the races followed by dinner and drinks... There's a theme there... But all of these events had us coming away stronger than ever before. They'd be competitive, there would be banter and disagreements, there'd be stories to tell for months to come and, although we were a very mixed team of personalities, everyone had each other's back. A huge amount of that loyalty and sense of team came from these events, which would always be a combined team activity, preferably with some competition, an opportunity for something to end up a story and sharing food and drinks.

Chapter 16

Best memories

Many of the team leaders and marketing directors I spoke to told me some of their best memories and biggest successes in team building weren't formed in the office but around days like these. Many of them, including me, stayed in touch with team members they worked with 30 years ago because these bonds grew so strong.

Many WFA companies arrange their team meetings in restaurants, fully aware that the mixture of sharing food and drink is a natural bonding mechanism and one that most of us find hugely socially rewarding.

It doesn't always have to include food and drink obviously. David Fenton told me one of the best remembered events from his time as Marketing Director of the UK's best supplier of building materials was taking his team to the local fire brigade in North Hampton for the day where they role-played certain scenarios with the fire fighters. This really helped build team trust, he told me, as well as being an event that was talked about for many years. He said: *"You go into a smoke-filled room where you won't be able to see anything and as a team you have to go and rescue somebody in that smoke-filled room. It takes you out of your normal environment and puts you together totally out of your comfort zone. A shared experience that truly benefited the whole group."*

David also told me about the 'Annual Jaunt' – a charity walk where a group of team members would raise money for good causes over a week-long period. He explained: *"We're doing a good thing in terms of charity funding, but also as a team some of the memories that we got from that are just fantastic. We created a montage and I've still got the photo boards at home. We built some really good bonds and as a high-performing team we delivered great results on the back of that."*

So, to lead with empathy in a non 9 to 5 office environment we need to overhaul our communication and create a strategy that suits our team, what we do and how we do it.

Communication is the major shift in approach that all leaders have to plan, embrace and adapt for the non 9 to 5 world. The understanding that not everyone is in the same place at the same time all the time is key. We need to inform often and succinctly enough but without overuse of tech and risking the team drowning in information overload. We need to check in with individuals more often and help our team keep communicating when we're not around.

We need more empathy as to when people are available and we need to respect people's non-work time and actively encourage no work-related communication outside of hours. But we shouldn't fear the lack of daily physical interaction. Regular contact with physical face-to-face sessions that combine collaboration and planning with food, drink and fun experiences can grow bonds just as easily as daily face-to-face nods when passing desks.

Chapter 16

Conclusion

In the introduction, I said that leading with empathy is the only way forward in our new, non 9 to 5 working world. Hopefully, after having read the book, you can now see just why empathy is such an essential skill for leaders to embrace themselves and to instil in their teams.

Over the course of this book we have explored what it means to be an empathetic leader and the people I interviewed and I have shared many real-world examples that demonstrate the benefits that leading with empathy brings.

Making your team feel valued, understood and trusted has always been important, but in a world where we no longer necessarily spend time in the same physical space, it is more important than ever to show, as a leader, how much you value your team, that you understand their challenges and that you trust them to do their jobs and do them well.

Leading with empathy brings numerous benefits for you personally, in that you will need to spend less of your time micromanaging people and can therefore dedicate more of your time teaching and mentoring your team to help them develop new skills and their own self management.

There is also nothing better than being part of a working culture and environment where everyone thrives. Empathy is a key element of creating such a culture because it builds trust, and this is essential not only between you, as the leader, and your team but also between your team members themselves. This is how you develop exceptional levels of teamwork, which in turn will lead to outstanding levels of customer service. This feeds into high levels of customer retention and growth because your team members not only treat each other with empathy but your customers too.

In leading with empathy, you also create a culture that people want to be a part of. This makes it easier for you to attract new talent and, when you hire with empathy, you are more likely to find the right fit people to become part of your team.

Empathy is the common thread that ties all of this together, which is why it is the most important leadership skill you can develop in the modern world, especially with more of us working remotely, as part of hybrid teams or WFA than ever before.

As I've explained, it is perfectly possible to build a strong, trusting and cohesive team in the WFA world, provided you take the right approach and that will invariably involve empathy.

Whether leading with empathy was a new concept to you before you picked up this book, or one you have been following for years, I sincerely hope you have found some value and wisdom in what I have shared here.

What follows here is a scorecard to help you gauge whether or not you already lead with empathy, and to help you identify any areas where you could improve. You can refer back to this whenever you need to check in with yourself, and you can also use the following as a kind of checklist to guide your own and your team's development.

Score yourself between 1 and 5 for each of the following questions, using this scale:

Strongly disagree	Disagree	Don't know	Agree	Strongly agree
1	2	3	4	5

1. I clearly define expectations around working hours, location and flexibility in collaboration with my team. I don't risk a "suck it and see" approach.

1	2	3	4	5

2. I don't just default to the old ways simply because they seemed to work. I recognise that, without a clearly explained and demonstrable business reason as to why I am insisting on a certain working format, the business risks losing quality team members.

| 1 | 2 | 3 | 4 | 5 |

3. I consider and am prepared for what effect any decision will have on each and every individual.

| 1 | 2 | 3 | 4 | 5 |

4. I am open and transparent in every area of my operations.

| 1 | 2 | 3 | 4 | 5 |

5. I have developed a coaching and mentoring mindset alongside a listening and understanding one.

| 1 | 2 | 3 | 4 | 5 |

6. I appreciate that even though non 9 to 5 means me and my team have a greater potential for a fantastic work-life balance, I need a far greater focus on protecting my time, avoiding distractions, maintaining mental and physical fitness, building new habits and teaching my team to do the same.

1   2   3   4   5

7. I have used the shift in the working environment to re-establish my goals and focus and to harness the power of teaching my team the same.

1   2   3   4   5

8. I work with my team to examine exactly WHY we all get out of bed and turn up for work each day.

1   2   3   4   5

9. I give my team purpose, responsibility and value in everything they do.

1   2   3   4   5

10. I have established a recruiting procedure aligned to my business' WHY and culture.

1   2   3   4   5

11. I build trust and healthy conflict within the team through open and honest discussions, feedback and team exercises.

1   2   3   4   5

12. I have had a rethink about how we communicate and built a strategy that encourages constant two-way communication through clearly structured and repeatable methods that still allow natural and free-flowing conversations.

1   2   3   4   5

Finally, always ask yourself if you're genuinely being empathetic. Not soft, not weak, but truly understanding. We've all come through rapid and huge change both professionally and personally and it will be many years before normal, whatever that may be, returns to many people's lives. This is such an amazing opportunity for you to truly reinvent the way you lead and the team you build. By truly leading with empathy you will not only enjoy the journey but also make the journey of those around you truly enjoyable and rewarding too.

Take a look at how you scored yourself on each of the 12 points listed above. How did you do (be honest)? Are there any areas where you can see a need for improvement? If there are, go back to the relevant chapter and learn about the tools you can use to help you embrace the power of leading with empathy. I'm also here to help guide you, so use the QR code at the end of this section to access online resources and to contact me if you feel you would benefit from further guidance.

I'd love to hear your thoughts on how this new world is impacting your team and how you are overcoming the challenges and changes we're all facing. I'd also love to invite you to be a guest on my podcast to discuss more.

You can contact me by email at john@mcm.click or via our website at www.mcm.click/empathy where you can also find more resources and links to some of the tools mentioned in this book.

I look forward to meeting you soon.

Useful resources

Just as you encourage rules for frequency of checking email, establish clear ground rules as to how you use these communication tools as a team. For example, for extremely urgent queries phone me; for an informal question that is not time sensitive use Slack.

Coffee Roulette

Randomly pairs up team members for a 15-minute virtual coffee break coffee-roulette.com

Otter

For meetings where one or more members cannot attend, consider using Otter www.otter.ai, which transcribes to a pretty decent written script that can be quickly skim read or listened to in real time (or a sped up version!).

Slack

A great tool for instant messaging that shows which team members are online.

WhatsApp

Mobile texting and image sharing can be useful for light-hearted shares but may encroach too much into personal life. As a team, you decide.

Sanebox

Sanebox.com learns intelligently what may or may not be important to you (you train it by dragging emails between folders) and filters out the unimportant emails for you to check at the end of the day.

What's YOUR WHY

We carried out the whole session remotely and as the day progressed each group recorded all of their thoughts and key points from their conversations on virtual post-it notes using https://www.mural.co/. It's a great platform: intuitive and as close to putting real post-it notes on a wall as you can get virtually without the hassle of having to take them off again! Even the very act of each team organising their own board brought about some enlightening, if predictable, debate about who was most obsessed about making sure everything was perfectly lined up.

FORMAT TO DISCOVER YOUR COMPANY WHY

Our initial day session took the following format:
- Introductions and setting the context
- Example of a WHY story
- Task in pairs
- The Golden Circle
  (explaining the circle of How, Why & What)
- How the session will run

CONVERSATION – What's Your Contribution?

Intro

Breakout groups:

"In each of your stories, what was the specific contribution MCM made to the lives of others?"

Reporting Back:

gathering the themes from the above breakouts.

BREAK

CONVERSATION – What's Your Impact?

Intro

Breakout groups:

"What did the contribution of MCM allow others to go and do or be?"

Reporting Back:

capturing the impact stories from the above breakouts.

Draft a WHY statement

Intro

Breakout groups:

WHY Statement Exercise: the team was split into two for this final session and led by senior team members to attempt to draft a 'why' statement between them.

Reporting Back: Presenting the WHY Statements

Wrap up

Acknowledgements

I've always wanted to write a book. How hard can it be? Well, I'll never read one again without huge admiration for the effort and support needed to achieve it. If I hadn't told my family, friends, team, clients and network that I'd started, I doubt I'd ever have finished. So a massive thank you to everyone who supported me along the way.

The danger of thanking individuals is that you may miss someone out. Throughout the writing and whilst carrying on with the "day job", I had encouragement and advice from so many different people that I came into contact with every day, so if you helped me then a huge thank you to you – especially all those of you, too many to mention, who gave up their time to speak to me and shared some excellent wisdom on being the best team leader possible.

In particular, I am really grateful for those who have let me share their words within the book, including Kiran Haslam, at the time Chief Marketing Officer at Princess Yachts, a hugely inspirational man with so many incredible experiences to share. Tamara Littleton, CEO of The Social Element, who gave up her time to speak to me and really made me believe this whole WFA dream is both achievable and hugely good for team and business.

Mark Pearson for his stories about Egg, the first internet bank. David Fenton for sharing both past and present from Jewson to the Marketing Centre and reminding me just how our early career friendships endure forever. Hannah Poulton of the Marketing Centre, who has just completed her first half marathon but says, "quote still applies: it doesn't get any easier!". Tim Parrack of the Marketing Centre for introducing me to so many great contacts within his organisation.

Bruce Tip Poon – where do I start? Such a privilege to spend time with him and an absolute trailblazer in the world of building team cultures. An interview I'll never forget! Simon Timmis, of the Institute of Engineering, hugely busy at the time yet still finding the time to speak. Daniel Robey at Think Jam for still keeping the interview going even whilst he was on his way to get his vaccine, having been pinged with a last-minute appointment. Emily Cason, who has now moved on from Cats Protection but shared some great tips, especially something as simple yet effective as the About Me Manual. Stuart Miles, of https://www.pocket-lint.com/, for not only his team building knowledge but also his writing tips. It was also fantastic to interview someone whose website I have been a regular visitor to for nearly 20 years.

Louise Dell, owner of Kyero.com, whose absolute dedication to making her team happy and putting that at the centre of all she does was such a pleasure to hear. She's one of those people who makes the whole process of leading a team whilst also trying to be the best version of herself seem totally effortless, but I know a huge amount of work goes into all she does and all she continues to innovate.

Raman Verma, who owns the agency Kandidly.co.uk, for not only reading and helping with the draft version of this book, but also for continuously encouraging me to complete it and for the regular monthly meetings we continue to have just to keep each other sane in agency land.

Christine MacKay, of Salamandra.uk, who was inspired at the same time as me to finally write that book, yet is far braver and not the massive overthinker I am – so started and finished several months before me. Thank you, Christine, for helping me with the content, sharing your stories, inspiring me to keep getting up at silly o'clock to write it before the work day started, being a Beta reader and for your constant support on LinkedIn. If you get a chance, you should definitely read Christine's book, which will open your eyes to the huge potential of animation for B2B marketing: "Destination Animation: How smart marketeers convey complex messages memorably"[38]

---

[38] *Christine Mackay, (2021), Destination Animation: How smart marketeers convey complex messages memorably, Rethink Press*

Dr Jon Finn BA (Hons), MSc, PhD and founder of Tougher Minds, who genuinely helped to keep me sane during 2020. His course "Chief Habit Mechanic"[39] is such a hugely effective and simple-to-follow method for helping you be your best version; teaching it to others taught me so much in an area I thought I already knew plenty about. Over around six months of interactive learning, one-to-one sessions and building a series of "tiny habits", I really felt I had tamed my A.P.E. and was finally in a position to embark on training my team how to do the same without the constant feeling of imposter syndrome. I'd highly recommend enrolling in one of his courses and learning the science-backed methods he has taught some of the largest sports stars, teams and companies in the world.

My wife Theresa for putting up with the A.P.E. on those days when the combination of working, writing and contending with life's inevitable curve balls didn't always see me get the "best version" bit right. To my sons: Thomas, for making me realise that the subject matter of this book was what I was truly qualified to write about (it was nearly a book about Pay Per Click advertising!) and Adam, for reminding me 50,000 words wasn't much more than his university dissertation – how hard can it be?

---

[39] *Further details on Tougher Minds, Chief Habit Mechanic course available here: https://www.tougherminds.co.uk/chief-habit-mechanic-leadership-certificate/*

To the editing and publishing team Georgia, and Kat for sticking with me throughout and to Ivan for his calm and logical support throughout the editing process. To Faye Brown at fayebrown.co.uk for instantly getting what we wanted as a cover design for this book and making the process so easy.

And, of course, to my team – without them there wouldn't have been a book to write. A special thanks to Carl, Jo, Tom, Alyssa, Fern and Paige for reading the first draft, making suggestions, encouraging me when I could so easily have stopped and for generally being such a huge support at all times. We have an amazing team of hugely talented individuals but I can genuinely say, even more important than the talent is that all of them are genuinely decent, warm-hearted individuals. There's only so much that leadership can shape a team. A huge element is down to the individuals within it. I hope one day you'll get to experience the fantastic culture, service and talent first hand.

About the Author

John McMahon has made empathy a cornerstone in his leadership during his 25 years at the helm of the award-winning digital marketing agency MCM. His passion for putting team culture first in the belief that great results naturally follow started in his first job as a City of London broker back in the late '80s as part of a groundbreaking team that put team culture and relationships before anything else.

Over the past 25 years since leaving the city to form his digital marketing agency, MCM, his team have produced hugely successful marketing campaigns for companies such as the Financial Times, British Gas, Lidl, Cats Protection and a huge range of national and international businesses.

Having founded MCM the year before Google was born, he has constantly had to adapt the agency's services to deliver consistently great results. From basic websites, email marketing and viral games through to customer acquisition via paid media on channels such as LinkedIn, Google and TikTok, one area that hasn't changed is his belief in and passion for team building.

In this book, John combines the knowledge he's built and adapted during that journey with insights from some of his interviews with over 50 internal marketing team leaders, CEOs and business owners. The interviewees ranged from leaders of traditional teams to teams that have been remote or hybrid for many years.

Outside of agency life, John is a keen runner and has enjoyed running city marathons across the world. When he's not spending time travelling and exploring as many different cultures as he can with his wife Theresa, he can be found with his sons boating off the South Coast of England.

Printed in Great Britain
by Amazon